CERVANTES AND ARIOSTO

PRINCETON ESSAYS IN LITERATURE

For a list of titles in this series, see pages 151–53

Cervantes and Ariosto

RENEWING FICTION

By Thomas R. Hart

PRINCETON UNIVERSITY
PRESS

Copyright © 1989 by Princeton University Press
Published by Princeton University Press, 41 William Street,
Princeton, New Jersey 08540
In the United Kingdom: Princeton University Press,
Guildford, Surrey

Library of Congress Cataloging-in-Publication Data
Hart, Thomas R.
Cervantes and Ariosto : renewing fiction / Thomas R. Hart.
p. cm. — (Princeton essays in literature)
Bibliography: p.
Includes index.
ISBN 0-691-06769-4 :
1. Cervantes Saavedra, Miguel de, 1547-1616. Don Quixote.
2. Ariosto, Lodovico, 1474-1533—Influence—Cervantes.
3. Ariosto, Lodovico, 1474-1533. Orlando furioso.
4. Chivalry in literature. I. Title. II. Series.
PQ6353.H27 1989
863—dc19   88-28167

Publication of this book has been aided by the
Whitney Darrow Fund of Princeton University Press

This book has been composed in Linotron Granjon

Clothbound editions of Princeton University Press books
are printed on acid-free paper, and binding materials are
chosen for strength and durability. Paperbacks,
although satisfactory for personal collections,
are not usually suitable for library rebinding

Printed in the United States of America by
Princeton University Press,
Princeton, New Jersey

In memory of Erich Auerbach

CONTENTS

PREFACE

I began thinking about the subject of this book more than thirty years ago when I first read Erich Auerbach's *Mimesis*, which had just appeared in English translation. As a graduate student at Yale, I had attended Auerbach's classes on Dante and on the medieval romance lyric; he had served as one of the readers of my dissertation. I liked him and admired his book, though just how much there is to admire in it became clear to me only years later as I became better acquainted with his other writings and with more of the works he discusses in *Mimesis*. From the beginning, however, I was troubled by Auerbach's insistence that *Don Quixote* is not a serious, much less a tragic work, but a comedy. His claim went counter to much of the little I had then read about it.

I began by thinking that Auerbach had misunderstood Cervantes' masterpiece and then began to wonder why he had misunderstood it in this particular way. I finally came to see that he read *Don Quixote* in much the same way he read *Orlando furioso*. Repeated readings of *Don Quixote* in preparation for my classes on it over the next thirty years, together with greater familiarity with Ariosto's poem, finally convinced me that Auerbach came closer to defining the essence of *Don Quixote* than any other writer I know. This book is a wholly inadequate expression of my debt to him.

My own view of *Don Quixote* nevertheless differs from Auerbach's in many ways. I do not believe that it is really as free from political intention as Auerbach suggests. I think, too, that Cervantes' attack on the romances of chivalry is combined with an attack on a way of reading that he thought potentially dangerous whatever the precise nature of the books read. I see *Don Quixote* as a more serious work than Auerbach thought it was. Perhaps it would be better to say that I think its seriousness is not of the kind Auerbach saw in it. But I could hardly have written this book without the stimulus provided by his magnificent essay.

IN writing this book I have tried to keep in mind not only students of Spanish literature but also students of English and of comparative literature, for whom *Don Quixote* usually provides their first and often only contact with the literature of Spain. For this reason, I have not hesitated to repeat some things that will be familiar to Hispanists and have been generous in providing bibliographical references that will lead the reader to fuller treatments of many points touched on in passing. Since readers whose primary interest is in the development of modern fiction are unlikely to be familiar with *Orlando furioso*, I have tried to give some idea of its content and of its place in literary history.

Quotations from primary sources are given both in the original Spanish or Italian and in English; in a few cases where the sense is clear from the immediate context, only the original is given. Quotations from secondary sources are given only in English. Translations are my own unless otherwise noted. I have, however, consulted John Ormsby's translation of *Don Quixote* in the revised version by Joseph R. Jones and Kenneth Douglas and have often found there an elegant and accurate solution to problems I had found intractable. Guido Waldman's prose translation of *Orlando furioso* has helped me to see the exact sense of many passages, as have the excellent notes in Lanfranco Caretti's edition of the Italian text and those in the still more fully annotated edition by Emilio Bigi. Since no prose version can give even a faint idea of the grace and movement of Ariosto's ottava rima, I occasionally cite passages from Barbara Reynolds's superb verse translation in the Penguin Classics, which often succeeds in catching both the sense and the spirit of Ariosto's stanzas.

References to *Don Quixote* are to part, chapter, and page number in L. A. Murillo's edition; references to part 2 are to Murillo's second volume. References to *Orlando furioso* are to Lanfranco Caretti's edition and are to canto and stanza; if less than a stanza is quoted, line numbers within the stanza are added. References to Castiglione's *Book of the Courtier* are to book, chapter, and page number in Bruno Maier's edition of the Italian text. The bibliography lists all the works cited together with a few others, mostly primary sources, that I found useful but had no occasion to mention in the text.

ACKNOWLEDGMENTS

An earlier version of much of this book was presented as a course of undergraduate lectures at Oxford University in Hilary term 1986. I am grateful to my Oxford colleagues, in particular Professor Ian Michael, Dr. R. W. Truman, and F. W. Hodcroft, for making my stay there so pleasant and productive. Dr. T. F. Earle kindly proposed me as a Visiting Senior Member of his own college, Linacre. I owe a special debt of gratitude to P. E. Russell, Emeritus Professor of Spanish Studies at Oxford, for sharing with me his knowledge of Spanish literature and Spanish history and for many kindnesses over a period of more than twenty years. Professor Cecil Grayson, Dr. J. R. Woodhouse, and Marco Dorigatti, a research student, helped clarify my thinking about Ariosto. Giles Barber, the librarian of the Taylor Institution, and his assistant John Wainwright did everything possible to facilitate my work there.

Three colleagues at the University of Oregon, Raymond Birn, Roger Nicholls, and Steven Rendall, read all or a substantial part of the typescript. My text has benefitted also from the attention of Patricia Daniels, the able Production Editor of *Comparative Literature*. My wife Margaret has helped in innumerable ways, especially by sharing with me her knowledge of computers.

Two anonymous readers for Princeton University made a number of constructive suggestions. They have since identified themselves as Professor John J. Allen of the University of Kentucky and Professor Gerald Gillespie of Stanford University. My Princeton editor, Julie Marvin, has been meticulous, infinitely resourceful, and a delight to work with.

ACKNOWLEDGMENTS

Finally, it is a pleasure to acknowledge the help of the National Endowment for the Humanities, which supported my work on Cervantes with a Fellowship for Independent Study and Research.

CERVANTES AND ARIOSTO

INTRODUCTION

In his essay "Kafka y sus precursores," Jorge Luis Borges remarks that "every writer *creates* his own precursors. His work modifies our conception of the past just as it will modify the future" (1960, 48). Cervantes has served as a precursor, often a gratefully acknowledged one, for some of the greatest of later novelists. Fielding, Stendhal, Flaubert, Melville, Dostoevski, Joyce, and of course Kafka, as Marthe Robert (1977) has shown in a brilliant juxtaposition of *Don Quixote* and *The Castle*, have all contributed to our understanding of Cervantes' novel. In bringing *Don Quixote* closer to us, they have inevitably transformed it. The *Don Quixote* we read today is a very different book from the one Cervantes' first readers knew.

One way of getting closer to the book Cervantes' contemporaries read is to compare *Don Quixote* with the fiction that preceded it. Many scholars have examined Cervantes' relationship to earlier Spanish fiction, especially the romances of chivalry. The earlier narratives Cervantes knew were not, however, all written in Spanish. As a young man he spent several years in Italy, and he seems to have retained a special interest in Italian literature throughout his life. Nor was all the narrative fiction known to him written in prose. He certainly knew and admired Ariosto's chivalric romance in verse *Orlando furioso*, one of the great best-sellers of sixteenth-century Europe.

Cervantes' familiarity with *Orlando furioso* and his admiration for it are beyond question: he refers to Ariosto or his poem at least twenty times in *Don Quixote*. A comparison of *Don Quixote* with *Orlando furioso* offers several advantages over a comparison with the romances of chivalry. Although

3

there are very few demonstrable borrowings from *Orlando furioso* in *Don Quixote* aside from the interpolated novella "El curioso impertinente" (Chevalier 1966, 459), it seems likely that Cervantes learned more from Ariosto, whose work he admired, than from the Spanish romances of chivalry, most of which he despised. *Orlando furioso*, moreover, is well worth reading for its own sake. It is easily accessible, both in English and in excellent scholarly editions of the Italian text, while almost all the Spanish romances of chivalry can be read only in the original sixteenth-century editions, some of them now exceedingly rare. Finally, the numerous annotated editions of *Orlando furioso* published in the sixteenth century give a hint as to the way Ariosto's text was approached by some contemporary readers.

Cervantes may have been attracted to *Orlando furioso* by a feeling that Ariosto shared not only his own attachment to the moral code of chivalry but also his conviction that it could not be practiced effectively in the contemporary world. Even more important may have been a belief that Ariosto shared his awareness of the gap between life as it is lived and life as it is depicted in works of imaginative literature. Ariosto wittily mocks the fashionable chivalric literature of his day, and at the same time uses it as a point of departure for a richer and more subtle work. Cervantes certainly knew that *Orlando furioso* was a continuation of Boiardo's *Orlando innamorato*. Although he probably knew nothing about the *cantastorie*, the minstrels whose treatments of Carolingian legend supplied Ariosto with much of the raw material of his poem, he could not have failed to notice that Ariosto's poem was a parody of works very much like the romances of chivalry that he claims to attack in *Don Quixote*. Like Ariosto before him, and perhaps inspired by Ariosto's example, Cervantes rethinks both the narrative conventions and the moral basis of chivalric fiction.

4

Not just chivalric fiction, however. In *Don Quixote* Cervantes also rethinks the conventions of pastoral literature and subjects them to the same searching reappraisal he gives to chivalric romance. It is in his treatment of pastoral that Cervantes anticipates most clearly a course that was to be followed by many later novelists and departs farthest from the example of Ariosto, who touches on pastoral motifs only in passing. The pastoral affords Cervantes an opportunity to deal with a theme of central importance in *Don Quixote* that does not appear in *Orlando furioso*: the way books can change their readers' lives.

CHAPTER I
Erich Auerbach's *Don Quixote*

In the first edition of *Mimesis*, which appeared in German in Switzerland in 1946, Erich Auerbach discusses *Don Quixote* briefly in two different chapters. In the chapter on the chivalric romances of Chrétien de Troyes, he compares Don Quixote's first sally, which leads him to an inn that he takes to be a castle, to Calogrenant's journey in Chrétien's *Yvain*. The essential difference between the two journeys is that

> the world which Don Quixote encounters is not one especially prepared for the proving of a knight but is a random, everyday, real world. By his detailed description of the circumstances of his hero's life, Cervantes makes it perfectly clear [that Don Quixote] is the victim of a social order in which he belongs to a class that has no function.... Only upon such a man, whose life is hardly better than a peasant's but who is educated and who is neither able nor permitted to labor as a peasant does, could romances of chivalry have such an unbalancing effect. (1953b, 137)

Auerbach returns to *Don Quixote* at the end of the chapter on Shakespeare to explain why Cervantes' novel does not fall within the bounds of the special kind of realism whose history *Mimesis* undertakes to trace:

> Seldom, indeed, has a subject suggested the problematic study of contemporary reality as insistently as does Don Quixote. The ideal conceptions of a past epoch, and of a class which has lost its functions, in conflict with the

reality of the contemporary present ought to have led to a critical and problematic portrayal of the latter. . . . But Cervantes did not elaborate his work in this direction. (ibid., 332–33)

Auerbach prepared a separate chapter on Cervantes for the Spanish translation of *Mimesis* published in Mexico in 1951; the German original, "Die verzauberte Dulcinea," appeared in a German scholarly journal in the same year. In the Spanish translation, and in subsequent editions and translations of *Mimesis*, the new chapter follows the chapter on Shakespeare. In the new chapter Auerbach refers to the "sociological and psychological interpretation" of *Don Quixote* that he had offered in his chapter on Chrétien and says that he "leave[s] it there because in the context of that passage it is justified." He now insists, however, that "as an interpretation of Cervantes' artistic purpose it is unsatisfactory, for it is unlikely that he intended his brief observations on Don Quixote's social position and habits of life to imply anything like a psychological motivation of the knight's idée fixe" (ibid., 348). Auerbach finds little in *Don Quixote* that deserves to be called tragic or problematic—one of his favorite words—because "Don Quixote's idée fixe saves him from feeling responsibility for the harm he does, so that in his conscience too every form of tragic conflict . . . is obviated. He has acted in accordance with the rules of knight-errantry and so he is justified" (ibid., 346). Auerbach thus sees *Don Quixote* as "a comedy in which well-founded reality holds madness up to ridicule" (ibid., 347), a work whose dominant mood is one of "merry play," "unproblematic gaiety" (ibid., 354).

Auerbach's essay on *Don Quixote* may be seen as an elaboration of the reasons that led him to treat Cervantes' novel so briefly in the original edition of *Mimesis*. He recognized Cervantes' originality in juxtaposing very different stylistic levels for comic effect: "What had certainly never happened before was that [such a rustically boorish style as that of the peasant woman's reply to Don Quixote in 2.10.110] should follow directly upon a speech like Don Quixote's—a speech which, taken by itself, could never make us suspect that it occurs in a grotesque context" (ibid., 350). He also recognized the uniqueness of Cervantes' achievement in creating a work that had no real precursors and has had no real descendants: "So universal and multilayered, so noncritical and nonproblematic a gaiety in the portrayal of everyday reality has not been attempted again in European letters. I cannot imagine where and when it might have been attempted" (ibid., 358). It was this uniqueness that made Auerbach feel that *Don Quixote* had nothing to do with the particular kind of realism that he deals with in *Mimesis*, "representations of everyday life in which that life is treated seriously, in terms of its human and social problems or even of its tragic complications" (ibid., 342).

Neither of Auerbach's two interpretations of Cervantes' novel fits easily into one of the two categories into which Oscar Mandel divides modern critics of *Don Quixote*. Mandel's "hard" critics consider Don Quixote the butt of Cervantes' satire, a madman unwilling or unable to see the world as it is. His "soft" critics stress the sublimity of Don Quixote's motivation and see his failure to impose his ideals as an indictment of the other characters and of the world in which the action takes place: "The knight is seen variously as the embodiment of the 'ideal' ... , the ethical life, the romantic life, the life of the imagination, poetry, heroism, or the rights of the individual" (1958, 154). Auerbach was, of course, familiar with the soft view as it was formulated by the German Romantics, and he goes out of his way to say that it is not supported by Cervantes' text. The interpretation he advances

in his chapter on Chrétien de Troyes differs from the romantic one in that Auerbach does not stress Don Quixote's nobility of character but rather the social and political conditions
that lead him to seek refuge in the imagined world of his
beloved books of chivalry. The interpretation offered in the
later chapter on *Don Quixote* is closer to those of Mandel's
hard critics, but Auerbach differs from them by denying that
Cervantes condemns Don Quixote as an irresponsible ide-
alist: he is simply a madman and therefore cannot be held
accountable for his actions. His adventures never go beyond
a harmless form of make-believe marked by a childlike in-
nocence of the real world.

Auerbach did not deny the greatness of *Don Quixote*,
though he understood its greatness differently from most
post-Romantic readers. *Mimesis* is not a history of Western
literature, still less an account of all the books Auerbach loved
or that he thought important. He found no place in it for a
number of authors he admired—for example, Vico, Pascal,
and Baudelaire, whose works he studied in some of his most
penetrating essays. In "Epilegomena zu *Mimesis*," Auerbach
notes that he has been accused of giving insufficient attention
to German writers. He concedes that the great French novelists of the nineteenth century—Stendhal, Balzac, Flaubert,
Zola—are given a central place in his book and that he
admires them enormously, but he insists that he treats them
in this way because of the special character of the problems
he deals with in *Mimesis* and not because of any personal
preference for their works over those of their German contemporaries. He adds that "for pleasure and refreshment [*zu
Vergnüge und Erholung*] I prefer to read Goethe, Stifter and
Keller" (1953a, 14). One reason he preferred them is perhaps
that they, especially Stifter and Keller, offer a vision of a
world still largely untouched by the tremendous historical

events that were to have such tragic consequences in Auerbach's lifetime and so decisive an effect on his own life. I suspect that his affection for Cervantes may have rested on a similar basis. There is no hint of condescension in his statement that "for Cervantes, a good novel serves no other purpose than to afford refined recreation, *honesto entretenimiento*. No one has expressed this more convincingly in recent times than W. J. Entwistle in his book on Cervantes ... where he speaks of recreation and connects it very beautifully with re-creation" (1953b, 358). Auerbach's pairing of recreation and re-creation here comes very close to his pairing of *Vergnüge* and *Erholung* in the passage just quoted. *Erholung* connotes rest, recovery, making whole again. Writing that can do this is hardly trivial, even if it is wholly unconcerned with everyday reality.

Why did Auerbach interpret *Don Quixote* in this way? The answer may lie in the expectations he brought to it, expectations formed by his university training in romance philology, a discipline to which he acknowledged his intellectual debt in the opening pages of the introduction, significantly titled "Purpose and Method," to his last, posthumously published book *Literary Language and Its Public* (1965, 5–6). Auerbach's university study of romance philology embraced the three principal romance languages and their literatures, but he devoted far less attention to Spanish literature than some other German and Austrian romance philologists like Karl Vossler or Auerbach's friend Leo Spitzer, to whom, in 1951, he dedicated his *Vier Untersuchungen zur Geschichte der französischen Bildung*. Spitzer made important contributions to the study of a number of major Spanish writers and works, among them the *Poema de Mio Cid*, the *Libro de buen amor*, the ballads, Garcilaso, Góngora, Quevedo, Lope de Vega, Calderón, and, of course, Cervantes. Auerbach's only extended discussion of a Spanish text aside from *Don Quixote* is his analysis, in *Literary Language*, of Juan Ruiz's lament for Trotaconventos in the *Libro de buen amor*, though there are scattered references to the Spanish theater of the Golden Age in *Mimesis* and perfunctory remarks on a number of Spanish works in the *Introduction aux études de philologie romane* that he prepared for his Turkish students. He was far more at home with French and Italian literature.

Auerbach's interpretation of *Don Quixote* may have been shaped in part by a tendency, perhaps largely unconscious, to see it in terms of one of the Italian books he knew and loved, Ariosto's *Orlando furioso*. In the handbook written for his Turkish students, Auerbach asserts that "reading [*Orlando furioso*] is one of the greatest pleasures offered us by European literature." He praises Ariosto as "the greatest epic poet of the Renaissance and one of the most purely artistic poets of all times," one whose work has "no other end than aesthetic pleasure" (1949, 150–51).

The last phrase suggests that Auerbach saw Ariosto in much the same light as he saw Cervantes. Ariosto appears in *Mimesis* only in passing—reasonably enough, given Auerbach's conception of realism—and almost always together with the author of *Don Quixote*. In his chapter on chivalric romance, Auerbach declares that "it is in the serene metamorphosis or the parody, Ariosto or Cervantes, that this fictitious form of life finds its clearest interpretation" (1953b, 140). In the chapter on Cervantes, he says that "I take [*Don Quixote*] as merry play [*heiteres Spiel*] on many levels, including in particular the level of everyday realism. The latter differentiates it from the equally unproblematic gaiety [*problemlose Heiterkeit*] of let us say Ariosto" (ibid., 354). On the next page he speaks of "the older tradition of the romance of adventure and its renewal through Boiardo and Ariosto," insisting that "no one before [Cervantes] had infused the element of genuine everyday reality into that brilliant and purposeless play of combinations."

The phrases that Auerbach's American translator Willard R. Trask renders as "merry play" and "unproblematic gaiety" are linked in the original German text by forms of the root *heiter*: *heiteres Spiel, problemlose Heiterkeit*. English offers no real equivalent for *heiter*:

> *Heiter* is applied to a state of mind which manifests itself inwardly more than outwardly and which is unclouded, serene. It can be applied to the higher activities of the mind, e.g. art (e.g. *die Heiterkeit der klassischen Kunst*), and also to its state in relation to everyday tasks and events. In the first case "serene," "bright" must often be used in English for lack of closer equivalents. In the latter case it approximates to "cheerful." Common to both *heiter* and "cheerful" are harmony and balance. (Farrell 1977, 214)

Serenity was a quality Auerbach valued highly, as I have pointed out elsewhere (Hart 1984, 1:260–61). He does not see *Don Quixote* merely as a comic work but as a comic work of a specific and uniquely valuable kind, a work wholly different in spirit from the crude slapstick to which Cervantes' contemporaries, both in Spain and abroad, seem generally to have reduced it (Russell 1969; 1985; Close 1978). Auerbach's essay is a triumph of imaginative insight, deeply rooted in both scholarly and personal concerns. Though questionable on certain points, it is, taken as a whole, the most satisfactory essay on *Don Quixote* that I know. It is tempting to suppose that Cervantes would have recognized it as a sympathetic and perceptive account of his work. But there is no evidence that Cervantes or his seventeenth-century readers interpreted *Don Quixote* as Auerbach does. Auerbach was right to reject as unhistorical the romantic view of Don Quixote as "a heroic defender of noble ideas in the face of all those who are ready to settle for the commonplace shallowness of things as they are" (Russell 1985, 94–95), but his own interpretation is hardly less unhistorical.

"Serene metamorphosis," "unproblematic gaiety," a "brilliant and purposeless play of combinations": all apply equally in Auerbach's view both to *Don Quixote* and to *Orlando furioso*. In seeing *Orlando furioso* in this way, Auerbach follows in the footsteps of De Sanctis and Croce, who set the tone for most criticism of Ariosto's poem in the first half of this century. De Sanctis, as C. P. Brand notes, "forces Ariosto into the pattern of his historical view of Italian literature, in which the Renaissance is condemned as abdicating moral responsibility with its cult of pure form, and the *Furioso* is seen as the masterpiece of art for art's sake" (1974, 192). Croce believed that Ariosto's art is concerned above all with harmony; the unity of his work is given by his irony, which is "similar to the eye of God, who watches creation moving, all creation, loving it all equally, in good and in evil, in the greatest and in the smallest, in man and in the grain of sand, because he has made it all" (quoted in English in Durling 1965, 250).

Though recent critics have laid increasing stress on Ariosto's fundamental moral seriousness and on his concern with the calamitous situation of an Italy ravaged by warfare between opposing city-states and by repeated foreign invasions, some of the most perceptive continue to find in *Orlando furioso* something of the serenity and gaiety Auerbach found both in Ariosto's poem and in *Don Quixote*. Lanfranco Caretti, for example, says that Ariosto's "wisdom rested on a serene and cordial openness toward the world [*un'apertura serena e cordiale verso il mondo*], which was based on a knowledge of man, of his various and even contradictory nature, and on an acceptance of reality in all its aspects" (1981, xviii).

Emilio Bigi speaks of the "achieved serenity" (*conquistata serenità*) of *Orlando furioso* and sees it as the quality that makes Ariosto's poem the most representative creation of its age and links it to the works of contemporaries like Raphael and Castiglione (1982, 1:66). Maxime Chevalier (1966, 460) suggests that the quality Cervantes most appreciated in Ariosto's poem was its "serene wisdom" (*sereine sagesse*).

In an influential article some years ago Giorgio De Blasi cited Ariosto's lines "Oh sommo Dio, come i giudicii umani / spesso offuscati son da un nembo oscuro!" (10.15.1–2) (Great God, how often human judgments are veiled by a dark cloud), and noted that the poet does not say *sempre*, "always," but *spesso*, "often," and elsewhere in similar contexts says *le piú volte*, "usually." He might equally well have cited "ecco il giudicio uman come spesso erra!" (1.7.2), perhaps the most frequently quoted line in the whole poem, which Barbara Reynolds renders, "See now how often human judgment errs!" De Blasi insists that Ariosto "is by no means a pessimist about life, for all his awareness of the errors of human desire" (1952–53, 335). Man's situation is not hopeless, because he possesses what Ariosto calls the light of reason, "[i]l lume del discorso" (7.2.4). Observing that Ariosto believes strongly in man's freedom to make proper use of his reason (ibid., 348) De Blasi calls him the poet of living well, one who believes fervently in the possibility of happiness in this world, a happiness certainly limited but nevertheless quite real (ibid., 354). Though Ariosto recognizes the futility of the constant struggle for happiness that engages all his characters, he does not despise them but on the contrary loves them precisely *because* they are deluded and inconstant.

I have paraphrased De Blasi at such length not only because his views are representative of some of the best modern criticism of *Orlando furioso* but also because I believe that they apply in large measure also to *Don Quixote*. Cervantes, too, knows that men do not always, or perhaps even often, act reasonably, but he does not draw the pessimistic conclusion that they can never do so.

Toward the end of his essay on *Don Quixote* Erich Auerbach attempts to define "the 'something' which orders the whole and makes it appear in a definite, 'Cervantean' light" (1953b, 355). He concludes that

> It is not a philosophy; it is no didactic purpose.... It is an attitude—an attitude toward the world and hence also toward the subject matter of his art—in which bravery and equanimity play a major part. (ibid., 355)

> The theme of the mad country gentleman who undertakes to revive knight errantry gave Cervantes an opportunity to present the world as play in that spirit of multiple, perspective, non-judging, and even non-questioning neutrality which is a brave form of wisdom. (ibid., 357)

Cervantes' admiration for *Orlando furioso* may have rested on a conviction that Ariosto shared a similar view of the world.

CHAPTER II

Cervantes' Debt to Ariosto: Form

Orlando furioso first appeared in print in 1516 in Ferrara, where Ariosto, then forty-two, was in the service of the Duke of Este. He had begun work on the poem at least ten years before. A second version, also in forty cantos but revised to make its language conform more closely to Tuscan usage, appeared in 1521. The definitive third version, which appeared in October 1532, only a few months before Ariosto's death, added six new cantos and incorporated further stylistic revisions prompted by the appearance in 1525 of Bembo's *Prose della volgar lingua*. *Orlando furioso* was reprinted more than a hundred times before the end of the century; by then it had been translated into all the major languages of Western Europe. Ariosto's poem was more than just a popular success. It rapidly attained the status of a classic, published in annotated editions with the same kind of moralizing commentary then given to Virgil and Ovid (Allen 1970, 283–86). It also became the focus for a long series of discussions of the aesthetic merit of the chivalric romances and their relationship to classical epic (Forcione 1970, chapter 1).

Orlando furioso was as popular in Spain as in Italy. Maxime Chevalier has given an excellent account of its reception by Cervantes' countrymen (1966). The first Spanish translation, by Jerónimo de Urrea, was published in Antwerp in 1549 (the first English version, by John Harington, did not appear until 1591) and was frequently reprinted; Chevalier lists eleven other sixteenth-century editions (1966, 504–05). In one of these, published in Venice by Gabriel Giolito in 1553, each

canto is preceded by an *argumento* that summarizes the action
and followed by an *alegoría* that sets forth the moral lessons
to be drawn from it. The volume also includes a list, taken
from Lodovico Dolce's Italian edition, of passages imitated
from classical writers and a "Tabla general por via d'alpha-
beto de las cosas mas notables que se contienen en el presente
libro," which corresponds to the alphabetical lists of characters and their actions found in modern scholarly editions like
those of Lanfranco Caretti and Emilio Bigi and in the English translations by Barbara Reynolds and Guido Waldman.
Another verse translation, by Hernando de Alcocer, was published in Toledo in 1550, and a prose translation by Diego
Vázquez de Contreras appeared in Madrid in 1585. These,
however, did not enjoy anything like the popularity of
Urrea's often-reprinted translation; neither reached a second
edition.

Many Spanish writers, like Cervantes himself, or rather
like Don Quixote's friend the priest, who presumably speaks
for his creator (1.6.114), probably preferred to read Ariosto in
Italian. The influence of *Orlando furioso* is evident in some of
the most important writers of Spain's Golden Age. Garcilaso
de la Vega incorporates material from it in all three of his
Eclogues. Both Garcilaso in his Second Eclogue and Alonso
de Ercilla in his epic poem *La Araucana* remind us that for
many sixteenth-century readers, *Orlando furioso* was a model
of heroic poetry rather than a masterpiece of comic writing.
Góngora chose an incident from Ariosto's poem as the point
of departure for "Angélica y Medoro", one of his most attractive works, and Ariosto's skittish heroine reappears as one of
the central figures of Lope de Vega's poem *La hermosura de
Angélica*.

William Nelson has noted that

parody is a remarkably common mode in the Renaissance. *Orlando furioso* and *Don Quixote* mock the chival-

17

ric tradition; *The Praise of Folly*, the rhetorical; *Gargan-tua*, the stories of giants; *Utopia*, the travelers' tales. None of these is merely parody, and in all but the *Or-lando*—perhaps I should not except it—the light fiction is made to carry a burden of weighty matter. This did not trouble contemporary readers, but it does confuse modern ones; the debate continues as to whether these works are witty entertainments or grave discourses. That they can be both at once seems to be hard for the modern reader to accept. (1973, 72)

Cervantes may have been less inclined than Nelson to doubt that *Orlando furioso* was both a witty entertainment and a grave discourse. He was committed to an aesthetic that demanded that literature be not only amusing but also morally responsible: fiction must instruct as well as delight (Riley 1962, 81–88). The annotated editions of *Orlando furioso* must have helped to confirm his belief that Ariosto's poem was morally serious.

I do not mean to suggest that Cervantes would have accepted all the allegorical teachings that the sixteenth-century commentators discovered in *Orlando furioso*. The commentaries amply confirm Paul J. Alpers' statement that "the allegorization of Ariosto was a fairly mindless process" (1967, 160; see also Salza 1914, 245–58). But if the allegorizers often did their job badly, it is easy to see why they thought it needed doing. *Orlando furioso* contains a number of passages that clearly demand allegorical interpretation, like Ariosto's account of Alcina's island in cantos 6 and 7, a reworking of the Circe legend. Sometimes the allegorical interpretation is present in the text itself, as in the allegory of fame that Saint John explains to Astolfo in canto 35.

Quite apart from passages that may or must be allegorized, and despite an abundant display of comic invention, Ariosto's poem is not a frivolous or escapist work. It abounds in instances of heroic behavior. The young Moorish soldier Medoro, determined to return to the battlefield under cover of darkness to search for the body of his lord Dardinello, is accompanied by Cloridano, who refuses to allow his friend to undertake such a dangerous mission alone (18.168–71). Isabella tricks Rodomonte into killing her so that she can be reunited with her dead lover Zerbino (29.13–26). The underlying ethical seriousness of *Orlando furioso* is an integral part of the text itself. Cervantes must have been as responsive to that seriousness as he was to Ariosto's sense of fun and his imaginative exuberance. He needed no commentator to point it out to him. And surely he would have rejected the reductive and platitudinous moralizing that is the allegorical commentator's stock-in-trade. The annotated editions of *Orlando furioso* must nevertheless have strengthened Cervantes' sense of the aesthetic dignity and the moral seriousness of Ariosto's poem. They must have helped to assure him that this poet for whom he surely felt a deep temperamental affinity was a thoroughly respectable model.

The opening stanzas of *Orlando furioso* set forth the three principal themes of the poem: first, the invasion of France by the Moorish king Agramante and the attempt of the Christian forces, led by Charlemagne, to drive him out again; second, the madness of Charlemagne's nephew Orlando when he discovers that Angelica, daughter of the Emperor of Cathay, has deserted him for a common soldier; and third, the exploits of the pagan champion Ruggiero, which culminate in his conversion to Christianity and his marriage to Bradamante. As founders of the house of Este, and thus forebears of the lords of Ferrara who were Ariosto's patrons, Ruggiero and Bradamante link the fictional world of the poem to the real world of Ariosto's first readers.

The three themes are loosely interwoven, and long stretches of the poem are no more than tangentially attached to any of them. Orlando himself, though he gives his name to the poem, is not even mentioned in several cantos. Most of the characters appear only briefly, when their paths cross those of others whose relationship to the themes is hardly more central than their own. "The formula," as C. S. Lewis writes of Ariosto's predecessor Boiardo, "is to take any number of chivalrous romances and arrange such a series of coincidences that they interrupt one another every few pages" (1936, 300). Ariosto's fondness for weaving several stories together rather than telling them one at a time is part of the heritage of medieval romance still very much alive in many of the masterpieces of Renaissance literature (Tuve 1966, 362–70; Vinaver 1971, 68–98; Delcorno Branca 1973).

Ariosto's sixteenth-century commentators say very little about his use of a multiple plot, though they devote a great deal of attention to the poem's unity, or lack of it. Some of them censure Ariosto on the ground that Aristotle had insisted that epic, like tragedy, is first of all an imitation of an action. For Aristotle, the best plots imitate a single action: "unity of plot does not, as some persons think, consist in the unity of the hero. For infinitely various are the events in one man's life which cannot be reduced to unity; and so, too, there are many actions of one man out of which we cannot make one action" (*Poetics* VIII, trans. S. H. Butcher).

In *Orlando furioso*, however, Ariosto presents a great many different actions not even tied together by being performed by the same person. Ariosto's contemporary champions defend him by arguing that Aristotle's precepts, however valid in his own time, are not universally binding. Giovambattista Giraldi Cintio, for example, in his *Risposta a M. Giovambattista Pigna* (1554), maintains that Ariosto did not set out to write an epic but a romance. He did not propose to treat a single action performed by a single knight, "vna sola attione di vn cavaliero," as Homer and Virgil had done, but sought instead to present many different actions performed by many men, "molte di molti" (quoted in Weinberg 1961, 2:960). The implication is clearly that a romance should be judged by its own rules, and not by those Aristotle had derived from the Homeric poems.

In another work, *Discorsi intorno al comporre dei romanzi*, also published in 1554, Giraldi Cintio argues in addition that Ariosto's use of a multiple action enabled him to "remove the satiety caused in the reader by reading always about one and the same thing," "leuare la satietà al lettore di sempre leggere una medesima cosa" (quoted in Weinberg 1961, 2:969). In stressing variety, Giraldi Cintio adopts a criterion repeatedly invoked by Ariosto, who often justifies one of his many shifts from one to another component of his wonderfully intricate plot "since I mustn't always say the same thing," "perché non convien che sempre io dica, / né ch'io vi occupi sempre in una cosa" (8.21.5–6).

Ariosto's favorite image for expressing the importance he attaches to variety is that of the weaver who needs many different threads. He first introduces it in canto 2:

> ma perché varie file a varie tele
> uopo mi son, che tutto ordire intendo,
> lascio Rinaldo e l'agitata prua,
> e torno a dir di Bradamante sua. (2.30.5–8)

(But since I need different threads for different parts of my tapestry, and I intend to weave them all together, I now leave Rinaldo and his tossing boat and turn back to his sister Bradamante.)

Ariosto returns to the same image when he insists that "Di molte fila esser bisogno parme / a condur la gran tela ch'io lavoro" (It seems to me that I need many different threads to complete my great tapestry) (13.81.1–2). In his first published work, the pastoral novel *La Galatea*, Cervantes uses the same word, *tela*, with reference to *Orlando furioso* when Calliope

21

says that it was she who helped Ariosto weave his varied and beautiful fabric, "soy la que ayudó a tejer al divino Ariosto la variada y hermosa tela que compuso" (422). In *Don Quixote*, the priest refers to "the invention of the famous Matteo Boiardo, with which the Christian poet Ludovico Ariosto also wove his fabric," "la invención del famoso Mateo Boiardo, de donde también tejió su tela el cristiano poeta Ludovico Ariosto" (1.6.114). Elsewhere, the Canon of Toledo, after attacking the romances of chivalry for their lack of unity and proportion, concedes that a gifted writer might use the form to treat a wide variety of subjects and weave them together to form a single tapestry, "una tela de varios y hermosos lazos tejida" (1.47.567).

Cide Hamete Benengeli uses the same argument in part 2 of *Don Quixote* when he notes that part 1 included stories, like those of the Captive and the "Curioso impertinente," that have nothing to do with Don Quixote and Sancho (2.44.366). Cide Hamete makes a clear distinction between these stories and others, like the story of Marcela and Grisóstomo or those of Cardenio and Dorotea, in which Don Quixote is involved, if only peripherally. Modern readers are inclined to lump the two kinds of stories together and to call them something like interpolated novellas. They are inclined also to see the significance of the stories primarily in their relationship to the main plot involving Don Quixote and Sancho. Cervantes himself, however, in his many remarks on fiction, "gives no hint of concern with the more recondite species of unity—thematic and symbolic, as opposed to mere formal unity—which it has been fashionable to find throughout his works" (Riley 1962, 130). Similarly, none of the sixteenth-century Italian commentators on *Orlando furioso* attempt to defend Ariosto's use of a multiple plot by arguing that the various strands of the plot are intended to throw light upon one another (Chevalier 1966, 53).

Critical interest in multiple plots seems to begin only in 1935 with William Empson's brilliant chapter, "Double Plots," in his book *Some Versions of Pastoral*. It is hardly surprising that the first studies of Ariosto's use of a series of interlocking plots linked by their relationship to the major themes of the poem came from British and American scholars like D. S. Carne-Ross and Robert M. Durling.

Carne-Ross acknowledges his indebtedness both to Empson and to Francis Fergusson, who declares that

The most fundamental question one can ask about any work of art is that of its unity: how do its parts cohere in order to make *one* beautiful object? Aristotle's answer ... is that a play or poem can be unified only if it represents *one action*. ... What then are we to say of plays, like many of Shakespeare's in which several plots ... are combined?

Aristotle, of course, did not have Shakespeare's plays, but he did have Homer, who also combined many stories, many plot sequences, both in the *Iliad* and the *Odyssey*. And he recognized that Homer unified that more complex scheme by obeying the fundamental requirement of unity of action: (VIII.3): "... he made the *Odyssey*, and likewise the *Iliad*, to center round an action that in our sense of the word is one." Aristotle returns to this point in Chapter XXIII, where he takes up the epic. Lesser poets, he says, have tried to unify an epic by basing it upon one character, or one great historic event, like the Trojan War. Only Homer had the vision to discover one action in the wide and diversified material of his epics. The action of the *Iliad* (as the first lines suggest) is "to deal with the anger of Achilles." The action of the *Odyssey* is "to get home again," a nostalgic motive which we feel in Odysseus's wanderings, in

Telemachus's wanderings, and in Penelope's patient struggle to save her home from the suitors. The interwoven stories, each with its plot, are analogous; and in the same way the stories which Shakespeare wove together to make a *Lear* or a *Hamlet* are analogous: varied embodiments of one action. (1966, 19–20)

Though Fergusson's notion of analogous actions may owe more to the New Criticism of the 1950s than it does to Aristotle, it can help us to understand how Ariosto wove together the strands of the immense tapestry that is *Orlando furioso*. One of the things Cervantes may have learned from Ariosto is how to tell a complex story by means of a series of analogous actions. A. A. Parker has observed that in *Don Quixote* Cervantes "does not link episodes in a chain of cause and effect, but ... progressively varies the pattern of the episodes in order to communicate through this changing pattern the expanding ramification of the theme" (1956, 14). Cervantes' procedure is nevertheless quite different from Ariosto's. None of the characters in Ariosto's poem, not even Orlando himself, is given the kind of central role Cervantes assigns to Don Quixote and Sancho.

Ariosto establishes links of the most varied kinds between the stories that make up *Orlando furioso*. Sometimes an incident is repeated, with variations, by different sets of characters. The partial repetition of such episodes constitutes an essential part of their meaning.

William Empson's observations on the function of double plots in the Elizabethan theatre apply equally to *Orlando furioso*: "A situation is repeated for quite different characters, and this puts the main interest in the situation not the characters." Empson remarks that "one would expect this to come naturally to the Elizabethans, because their taste must partly have been formed on those huge romances which run on as great tapestries of incident without changing or even much stressing character ... ; any one incident may be interesting, but the interest of their connection must depend on a sort of play of judgment between varieties of the same situation" (1935, 54).

Ariosto sometimes uses his multiple plot in precisely the way Empson describes in order to show that different individuals placed in similar situations may behave in similar ways, as when Ruggiero repeats Astolfo's error in falling prey to the wiles of Alcina, despite Astolfo's warning. Rodomonte berates Doralice for her fickleness in rejecting him and choosing Mandricardo, but he forgets her as soon as he meets Isabella, and Ariosto insists that his behavior is typical:

> O degli uomini inferma e instabil mente!
> come siàn presti a variar disegno!
> Tutti i pensier mutamo facilmente,
> piú quei che nascon d'amoroso sdegno. (29.1.1–4)

(Oh weak, inconstant minds of men! How quick we are
to change our plans! We change all our thoughts easily,
especially those which spring from a lover's disdain.)

Sometimes, however, Ariosto uses his multiple plot to make precisely the opposite point. Two characters placed in essentially the same situation may behave in radically different ways. At the end of canto 10, for example, Ruggiero finds Angelica, naked and chained to a rock, about to be sacrificed to a sea monster, the orc. Ruggiero rescues her and is on the point of raping her, but while he is struggling to free himself from his armor, Angelica escapes by placing in her mouth the magic ring that renders her invisible. In the next canto, when Orlando similarly finds Olimpia about to be sacrificed to the orc, he frees her and kills the orc, unlike Ruggiero, who had merely wounded it. Orlando differs from Ruggiero even more obviously in that he treats Olimpia with exquisite courtesy.

One of Ariosto's favorite techniques for interweaving the strands of his complex tapestry is to make a sudden break in the narrative by switching from one set of characters to another, for example, when he leaves Ruggiero on Alcina's island eagerly anticipating the moment when the sorceress will come to his bed and shifts to Charlemagne, engaged in a desperate struggle with Agramante, and to Bradamante, about to set out in search of her wayward lover:

> Stava Ruggiero in tanta gioia e festa,
> mentre Carlo in travaglio et Agramante,
> di cui l'istoria io non vorrei per questa
> porre in oblio, né lasciar Bradamante,
> che con travaglio e con pena molesta
> pianse piú giorni il disiato amante,
> ch'avea per strade disusate e nuove
> veduto portar via, né sapea dove. (7.33)

(Ruggiero feasted joyfully, while Charlemagne and Agramante labored; I do not want to slight their story for his, nor to forget Bradamante. She mourned for many days the lover she had seen carried off on strange and unfamiliar paths, she knew not where.)

The rapid shift from one story to the other accentuates the contrast between the faithful Bradamante and Ruggiero, unmindful of his obligations both to his lord and to the woman who loves him, just as it reiterates the point, made repeatedly throughout the poem, that our desires often lead us in directions opposed to our own best interests.

Cervantes, too, sometimes juxtaposes episodes for ironic effect. After Don Quixote and Sancho have spent more than two hours searching in vain for Marcela, they settle down peacefully to have lunch in a grassy meadow beside a stream. Sancho has not bothered to hobble Rocinante, and the horse soon trots off to join a group of mares tended by some Galician hostlers who are resting nearby:

> Sucedió, pues, que a Rocinante le vino en deseo de refocilarse con las señoras facas, y saliendo, así como las olió, de su natural paso y costumbre, sin pedir licencia a su dueño, tomó un trotico algo picadillo y se fue a comunicar su necesidad con ellas. Mas ellas, que, a lo que pareció, debían de tener más gana de pacer que de él, recibiéronle con las herraduras y con los dientes, de tal manera, que a poco espacio se le rompieron las cinchas, y quedó sin silla, en pelota. (1.15.191)

> (It happened then that Rocinante took it into his head to have a romp with the lady mares, and as soon as he scented them he abandoned his usual gait and behavior, and, without taking leave of his master, set off at a brisk little trot to make his needs known to them. But they apparently were more interested in grazing than in anything else and received him so fiercely with heels and teeth that they soon broke his saddle girth and left him naked.)

The archaisms (*facas*, *ál*), the expressive diminutives (*trotico*, *picadillo*), and the disparity in stylistic level between the colloquial *refocilarse* and the awkward circumlocution "se fue a comunicar su necesidad con ellas" all serve to emphasize the absurdity of the situation. The archaisms link Rocinante to Don Quixote, who often resorts to them when he is making a deliberate attempt to speak like a knight-errant, while the desire that animates Rocinante marks the distance between the horse and his master, since Don Quixote's love for Dulcinea leaves no room for any such impulse, here significantly called a need (*necesidad*). The fact that the episode immediately follows the conclusion of the story of Marcela and Gri-

27

sóstomo suggests a further contrast between the natural desire felt by Rocinante and Marcela's unnatural refusal to concede that such a desire exists.

The speed with which Ariosto moves from one incident to another is matched by the speed with which he moves from high comedy to pathos or tragedy and then back again. D. S. Carne-Ross has argued persuasively that the juxtaposition of episodes that demand very different emotional responses from the reader does not undercut the intensity of the emotions themselves: "Orlando's loyalty to Angelica is touching and even noble; it is also quite ridiculous" (1966, 231). Surely one could say the same thing of Don Quixote's love for Dulcinea and, indeed, of his whole conception of knight-errantry.

Ariosto's fondness for making his reader jump from intense emotional involvement with the fate of a character to the detachment required for a comic or ironic view is matched by his delight in frequent shifts of stylistic level from stanza to stanza and even within a single stanza. His ottava rima underscores the rapid movement of his story and its freedom to go anywhere with dizzying speed, a freedom symbolized by Ruggiero's hippogriff and its counterpart the magic steed Rabicano, which allows Astolfo to move about the world as easily as Ruggiero. Italo Calvino suggests that

> The secret of Ariosto's octaves lies in their ability to catch the varied rhythms of spoken language ... ; but the colloquial register is only one of the many at his disposal, which go from lyric to tragic to gnomic and may coexist in the same stanza. ... The very structure of the octave rests on a break in rhythm: six lines bound together by a pair of alternating rhymes are followed by a rhyming couplet. We might call the effect one of anti-climax, an abrupt change not just in rhythm but in

psychological and intellectual climate, from the aristocratic to the popular, or from the evocative to the comic. (1970, xxv)

Ariosto often asserts his absolute control over the events of his narrative by interrupting the action at its most suspenseful point, as he does when he leaves Ruggiero struggling to remove his armor in his haste to ravish Angelica:

> Ma troppo è lungo ormai, Signor, il canto,
> e forse ch'anco l'ascoltar vi grava:
> sí ch'io diferrirò l'istoria mia
> in altro tempo che piú grata sia (10.115.5–8)

(But the canto is already too long, my lord, and perhaps you are tired of listening to it, so I will postpone my story until a more opportune moment.)

Cervantes similarly interrupts his account of Don Quixote's fight with the Biscayan on the pretext that his sources do not tell him how it turned out:

> Pero está el daño de todo esto que en este punto y término deja pendiente el autor desta historia esta batalla, disculpándose que no halló más escrito, destas hazañas de Don Quijote, de las que deja referidas. (1.8.137)

(But the difficulty is that at this very moment the author of the history leaves the outcome of the battle in suspense, excusing himself by saying that he found nothing more written about Don Quixote's deeds than has already been told.)

Authorial interventions of this kind, which remind us that we are reading a story and call attention to the author's role in shaping it, are comparable to Henry Fielding's frequent

29

insistence on speaking in his own voice in *Tom Jones*. Ian Watt says that Fielding's interventions create "a distancing effect" while keeping the reader aware of "the larger implications of the action" and offering the "responsible wisdom about human affairs" that Watt sees as Fielding's major contribution to the development of the novel (1957, 285, 288). All this is admirably said, and it is equally true of Cervantes, whom Fielding acknowledged as a model in *Joseph Andrews*. Watt fears, however, that what he calls Fielding's "realism of assessment" (ibid., 291) has been bought at too high a cost, since it interferes with "realism of presentation" (ibid., 290), which he finds in Samuel Richardson. Fielding's stylistic exuberance "diverts our attention from the content of the report to the skill of the reporter" (ibid., 30). His interventions "obviously interfere with any sense of narrative illusion, and break with almost every narrative precedent, beginning with that set by Homer, whom Aristotle praised ... for saying 'very little *in propria persona*' " (ibid., 286).

Watt exaggerates Fielding's break with narrative precedent. In fact, Fielding's authorial interventions place him squarely in the tradition of Cervantes—and, of course, of Ariosto. Robert Alter is closer to the truth when he asserts that Cervantes "is the initiator of both traditions of the novel; his juxtaposition of high-flown literary fantasies with grubby actuality pointing the way to the realists, his zestfully ostentatious manipulation of the artifice he constructs setting a precedent for all the self-conscious novelists to come" (1975, 3–4). Like Watt, Alter does not mention Ariosto; the tradition that interests him is limited to the prose fiction that follows *Don Quixote*.

Cervantes and Ariosto are not exceptional in refusing to try to persuade their readers that they write about people who really lived and things that really happened. As William

Nelson notes, "So far are some makers of Renaissance fiction from desiring to create a convincing illusion of reality that . . . they go about deliberately to sabotage it and to poke fun at those so simple as to entertain it" (1973, 68). All of the devices used by Ariosto and Cervantes to introduce variety into their narratives—the interruption of an episode just as it reaches its moment of maximum tension, the sudden shifts from one episode to another, the rapid changes in stylistic level—help to keep us aware that we are reading a story, not witnessing an action.

Our list of such devices could, of course, be greatly extended. Both Cervantes and Ariosto are fond of insisting on their fidelity to the historical record, though they make clear in doing so that their claims are not to be taken seriously. Ariosto sometimes cites conflicting versions of a single event, often wildly improbable in itself, as in his account of the hermit who provokes Rodomonte to kill him by arguing that Isabella should be allowed to carry out her plan to enter a convent:

> E sí crebbe la furia, che nel collo
> con man lo stringe a guisa di tanaglia;
> e poi ch'una e due volte raggirollo,
> da sé per l'aria e verso il mar lo scaglia.
> Che n'avenisse, né dico né sollo:
> varia fama è di lui, né si raguaglia.
> Dice alcun che sí rotto a un sasso resta,
> che'l piè non si discerne da la testa;
>
> et altri, ch'a cadere andò nel mare,
> ch'era piú di tre miglia indi lontano,
> e che morí per non saper notare,
> fatti assai prieghi e orazioni invano;
> altri, ch'un santo lo venne aiutare,

31

> lo trasse al lito con visibil mano.
> Di queste, qual si vuol, la vera sia;
> di lui non parla piú l'istoria mia. (29.6–7)

Barbara Reynolds captures Ariosto's tone with wonderful precision:

> His wrath and fury grew, till, like a vice,
> His hand had gripped the hermit's neck and throat;
> Then round his head he whirled him once or twice
> And flung him toward the sea; whether or not
> The holy man then paid the final price,
> Varies according to the anecdote:
> In one, his body struck against a stone
> And there, unrecognized, his parts were strewn.
>
> Some have suggested in the interim
> He fell into the sea, three miles away,
> And that he died because he could not swim:
> All he could do was clasp his hands and pray;
> Still others that a saint assisted him:
> A hand came out of Heaven to convey
> The drowning man ashore; howe'er it be,
> No more about him now you'll hear from me.

Cervantes similarly explains that his sources do not agree on the name of his protagonist:

> Quieren decir que tenía el sobrenombre de Quijada, o Quesada, que en esto hay alguna diferencia en los autores que deste caso escriben; aunque por conjeturas verosímiles se deja entender que se llamaba Quejana. Pero esto importa poco a nuestro cuento; basta que en la narración dél no se salga un punto de la verdad. (I.I.71)

(Some say that his surname was Quijada, or Quesada, for on this point there is some disagreement among those who write on the subject, although plausible conjectures suggest that his name was Quejana. But this is of little importance for our story; it is enough that in telling it we shall not stray a hair's breadth from the truth.)

Though both Ariosto and Cervantes often remind their readers that the work before them is a fiction, both also take care not to let them lose sight of the real world. Ariosto repeatedly juxtaposes the real and the fantastic, a practice that no doubt owes something to Dante's introduction of realistic details drawn from everyday life into the terrifying visions of his *Inferno*. When Ruggiero flies from Asia to England on the hippogriff, he is as much concerned with finding suitable lodging as any modern tourist:

> Non crediate, Signor, che però stia
> per sí lungo camin sempre su l'ale:
> ogni sera all'albergo se ne gía,
> schivando a suo poter d'alloggiar male. (10.73.1–4)

(You must not imagine, my lord, that he remained on the wing throughout so long a journey. He spent every night in an inn, avoiding poor accommodations as much as possible.)

Cervantes uses a variant of the same motif in Don Quixote's conversation with an innkeeper:

> Preguntóle [el ventero] si traía dineros; respondió don Quijote que no traía blanca, porque él nunca había leído en las historias de los caballeros andantes que ninguno los hubiese traído. A esto dijo el ventero que se enga-

ñaba: que, puesto caso que en las historias no se escribía por haberles parecido a los autores dellas que no era menester escrebir una cosa tan clara y tan necesaria de traerse como eran dineros y camisas limpias, no por eso se había de creer que no los trujeron. (1.3.89)

(The innkeeper asked him if he had any money with him. Don Quixote answered that he hadn't a penny, since he had never read in books of chivalry that any knight ever carried money. The innkeeper replied that he was mistaken, for, although nothing is said about it in the books, since their authors thought it unnecessary to mention anything so obvious and so essential to a traveler as money and clean shirts, nevertheless one must not assume that they did not carry them.)

Cervantes may have learned from *Orlando furioso* not only how to juxtapose contrasting episodes for ironic effect and how to tie together different strands of narrative material by shifting from one story to another at the moment of greatest suspense—a device he uses far less often than Ariosto. Much more importantly, he may have learned to use a multiple plot to make a single, extraordinarily rich thematic statement. Many critics have noted that Angelica's headlong flight through the wood to elude her pursuers in canto 1 prefigures the action of the whole poem, in which we see one character after another in hot pursuit of an object of desire. The nature of the object is immaterial; it may be a person, or a thing, or simply a desire for adventure. What is striking is the urgency of the pursuit. No one has expressed the frenetic quality of Ariosto's world better than Italo Calvino:

From the beginning *Orlando furioso* announces itself as the poem of movement, or rather announces the particular kind of movement that will run through it from beginning to end, a movement in broken lines, a zigzag movement. We could trace the general design of the poem by following the continual intersecting and diverging of these lines on a map of Europe and Africa but the first canto alone would be enough to define them; it is wholly made up of pursuits, wrong turnings, chance meetings, errors, changes in plans.... Our pleasure in the speed of the action is blended with a sense of the generous scale of its movement in space and time. (1970, xxiv)

Calvino emphasizes that this boundless rush of energy does not belong just to Angelica's pursuers but also to Ariosto himself as storyteller, "il movimento *errante* della poesia dell'Ariosto" (ibid., xxv).

I can think of no satisfactory translation for *errante*. The verb *errare* means both "to wander, roam aimlessly" and also "to err, go astray" in a moral sense, as in the General Confession in the Book of Common Prayer: "We have erred, and strayed from thy ways like lost sheep." Both senses are relevant in one of Ariosto's most often quoted lines, "Ecco il giudicio uman come spesso erra!" (1.7.2). Much of the action of the poem, the moral and physical trajectories of its major characters, is errante in this double sense. As Robert M. Durling observes, "All the characters ... are heedlessly pursuing some object of desire. They rush through the poem in pursuit of what turn out to be trivial and ultimately illusory goals. ... The madness of Orlando is simply the extreme form of what is universal" (1965, 164–65).

Durling's remarks are equally applicable to *Don Quixote*. Like Don Quixote himself, many characters in the novel— both major ones like Marcela, Grisóstomo, and Cardenio, and minor ones like Eugenio and Leandra—attempt to reshape their lives to make them conform to patterns learned from books. But the narrative pace of *Don Quixote* is much slower than that of *Orlando furioso*, in part because Cervantes makes so much use of direct speech in ways that do little to further the progress of the action.

Ariosto has a wonderful ability to fit the easy rhythms of vivid colloquial speech into the neatly packaged stanzas of his ottava rima, as in this exchange between Gradasso and Ruggiero:

> —Lascia la cura a me (dicea Gradasso),
> ch'io guarisca costui de la pazzia.—
> —Per Dio (dicea Ruggier), non te la lasso,
> ch'esser convien questa battaglia mia.—
> —Va indietro tu!—Vavvi pur tu!—né passo
> però tornando, gridan tuttavia. (27.66.1–6)

("Leave it to me," said Gradasso. "I'll cure him of his madness."

"By God," said Ruggiero, "I won't leave it to you. This battle was meant for me."

"Stand back!"

"Stand back yourself!"

And so they go on shouting, neither taking a step.)

Here the dialogue does not interrupt the action; it *is* the action. Certainly it does not slow the narrative. Similarly, in canto 9, stanzas 22–56, Olimpia's account of her misfortunes, though given in direct speech, is narrative in content and maintains the speed to which the rest of the poem has accustomed us. Ariosto's pace is, of course, not always the same. The tempo slows appreciably at certain moments, often those of highest emotional tension, for example, when Olimpia discovers that Bireno has abandoned her (10.23–34), or when Orlando struggles desperately to convince himself that Angelica has not left him for someone else (23.102–11). But

Orlando furioso offers nothing comparable to those moments when Cervantes brings the action almost to a standstill to let us overhear the marvelous conversations between Don Quixote and Sancho as they ride across the plains of La Mancha, that "long dialogue" that Gerald Brenan says

> suggests, in a more ceremonious key, the familiar dialogue of married couples. It is made up of the same inconclusive wranglings, the same recriminations and *tu quoques*, the same fixed recollections and examples dragged out again and again from the past to clinch an argument.... One of the most admirable things about this novel, which at first sight appears to be composed of separate episodes, strung together like beads on a thread, is that few things in it are really finished with when they have occurred. On the contrary, they are taken up into the minds of the two protagonists and reappear later on as a part of their argument.... It would be hard to find a novel in which the psychological repercussions of happenings had a greater importance. (1953, 183–84)

Ariosto's reader is often invited to consider the relationship between similar events, but his characters themselves do not do so. Usually, of course, they are not aware that they are repeating an episode already enacted by other characters. Ariosto admirably knits his narrative together in other ways, carefully completing all the stories left unfinished by Boiardo and making them integral parts of his own vastly more complex design, but *Orlando furioso* is in this respect more loosely constructed than *Don Quixote*.

Ariosto's repeated juxtaposition of the real and the fantastic serves to remind his readers that, as Durling observes, they are "not to rest in the world of the poem, but to look through it at the real world" (1965, 131). They are invited to compare the world of books with the real world in order to discover the limitations of both. Cervantes, too, juxtaposes the real world of early seventeenth-century Spain with the world of the romances of chivalry, though his treatment differs from Ariosto's in that his giants and enchanters exist only in Don Quixote's mind. They are products of Don Quixote's reading rather than of his experience; perhaps they reveal his lack of imagination, the "dry matter-of-factness" that Gerald Brenan suggests "may originally have led him, by its very dullness" to seek escape in his fantasies of knight-errantry (1953, 190). The poverty of Don Quixote's imagination may suggest also the poverty of the kind of books that nurtured it. The "real-life" adventures of Dorotea and Cardenio and the Captive are more exciting than the adventures Don Quixote creates from the scraps of experience that turn up in the course of his travels.

CHAPTER III

Cervantes' Debt to Ariosto:
Themes

E. C. Riley has speculated that "the artlessness and irresponsibility of many chivalresque novelists, and the contrast between their work and the *Orlando furioso*, for instance, might well have set [Cervantes] wondering about the principles of literary fiction" (1962, 6). Cervantes' reading of Ariosto may have done more than suggest some effective ways of telling a story. It may also have suggested the kind of story he wanted to tell in *Don Quixote*. Harry Levin's often quoted statement that throughout *Don Quixote* "there runs a single pattern: the pattern of art embarrassed by confrontation with nature" (1957, 79) is equally applicable to *Orlando furioso*. The pattern of art is in both cases formed by the conventions of chivalric romance, just as nature is the pattern of life in an early modern Europe still breaking away from its medieval past. Both *Orlando furioso* and *Don Quixote* examine the disparity between life as we experience it and life as it is depicted in books.

Any sweeping distinction between life and literature is, however, apt to be misleading where chivalry is concerned. Chivalry did not die with the end of the Middle Ages; indeed, its survival, or rather its revival, is one of the many links between the Middle Ages and the Renaissance increasingly stressed in recent scholarship. For Cervantes' contemporaries, as Martín de Riquer has noted, chivalry belonged to the real world and the very recent past: "knights-errant existed and still wandered the roads of Europe, from court to court, in search of adventures (jousts, passages of arms, tournaments, mortal combat) only a century before Cervantes began to write *Don Quixote*" (1973, 277).

The popularity of chivalry as a literary theme both in Spain and elsewhere cannot be explained solely by reference to literature itself. Rosemond Tuve has noted that "The *Faerie Queene* no longer stands so alone, as we consider plentiful evidence that the obsolescence of chivalry as an institution was far from obvious to a still partly feudal society, or evidence for the aristocracy's attempt to revitalize as well as to take refuge in the traditional ways of living and thinking" (1966, 341). Although it is certainly true that the decline of chivalry was not apparent to everyone, Ariosto and Cervantes surely perceived it.

Both Ariosto and Cervantes were intensely aware that chivalric values had been superseded though lip service continued to be paid to them. Ariosto reveals his awareness of the gap between chivalric ideals and actual behavior in his frequent addresses to his readers, and in the ironic asides that sometimes underscore the difference between the way his characters behave and the way they would behave if they were real people caught up in similar situations, and sometimes suggest instead that the "gran bontà de' cavallieri antiqui" (1.22.1) is as illusory in the world of the poem as it had become in sixteenth-century Italy. Cervantes reveals a similar awareness in setting Don Quixote's adventures in the prosaic everyday world known to his readers, for whom La Mancha had none of the picturesqueness since conferred on it by the passing of three centuries and above all by the success of *Don Quixote* itself.

Cervantes' evident sympathy for chivalric ideals even while he holds up to ridicule Don Quixote's attempt to revive them becomes easier to understand in the light of some recent studies in early modern European history. Frances Yates has demonstrated the importance of the "imaginative re-feudalization of culture" that took place all over Europe in the sixteenth century when "feudalism as a working social or military structure was extinct" (1975, 108). One of its manifestations was an increased interest in the institution of chivalry and in the imaginative literature devoted to it, an interest reflected in the popularity of *Orlando furioso* and the long series of reprintings and translations of Spanish romances of chivalry throughout the century.

The strengthening of interest in chivalry was favored by the personal tastes of the Emperor Charles V, the most powerful ruler in Europe. Charles had been duke of Burgundy before becoming king of Castile and Aragon in 1516 and, three years later, Holy Roman Emperor. His grandfather Philip the Good had founded the Order of the Golden Fleece, and Charles remained attached to the chivalric notions of his Burgundian ancestors throughout his life. In 1548 he replaced the traditional court ceremonial of the kings of Castile with that of the House of Burgundy, which made elaborate use of chivalric motifs. When Charles, accompanied by his son the future Philip II, visited the Flemish town of Bins in the following year, he was welcomed with lavish festivities dominated by chivalresque motifs, festivities remembered for years afterward (Devoto 1960; Heartz 1960).

The entertainment staged for Charles on his visit to Bins linked the chivalric ideal to the idea of world empire (Heartz 1960, 337–39), the foundation of Spanish foreign policy in the first half of the sixteenth century. The Imperial Court of the 1520s found strong support for the imperial ideal in the writings of Erasmus. Some Erasmian humanists, like Alfonso de Valdés, held important offices in the Imperial chancery. To them Charles' reign as Emperor seemed to offer a hope of establishing the universal peace that Erasmus saw as the indispensable first step in bringing about an undivided and reformed Christendom.

That hope was not realized. "After 1530," writes Hugh Trevor-Roper,

> after the climax of [Charles'] political success, the tide had begun to turn. Now no one believed in reform any longer. Erasmus was dead; the Erasmian vision had faded; the reforming Council of Trent had collapsed; military victory itself had been reversed. In the 1550s a disillusioned generation turned from reform to persecution. . . . The Emperor himself, in those years, came to regret his early tolerance, and though he continued to nourish old Erasmians at his court, and to read the works of Erasmus in private, he became a persecutor of heresy in his dominions. . . . After the fierce cautery of that terrible decade, the climate of Christendom could never be the same.
>
> Nor could its institutions. The imperial idea . . . had almost become a reality. . . . But now . . . its unreality had been revealed. It was an archaism, a mocking phantom from the past, which had briefly seemed embodied and then had dissolved again, never to be restored. Charles V was the last universal emperor, the last Emperor to be crowned by the pope. (1976, 39)

Charles remained attached to the ideals of his youth despite the collapse of his dream of world empire. Cervantes, too, seems to have remained attached to Erasmian ideals long after all of Erasmus' books had been placed on the Index. The influence of Erasmus on the *Novelas ejemplares* has been demonstrated by Alban Forcione, who asserts that "Cervantes's collection of exemplary tales . . . is perhaps Spain's most imposing tribute to the breadth of vision and generosity of spirit inspiring the Christian Humanist movement and distinguishing its enduring literary products" (1982, 21). Cervantes' work, writes Marcel Bataillon, "is that of a man who always remained faithful to the ideas he had learned in his youth, habits of thought that the age of Philip II had inherited from that of the Emperor" (1950, 2:401). But though Cervantes surely knew that he was out of step with his time, we should not exaggerate the gap between his ideas and those of some of his younger contemporaries. Bataillon is no doubt right to insist that "Cervantes captured in the atmosphere of contemporary Spain, rather than in the lessons of [his teacher] López de Hoyos, whatever diluted Erasmianism there is in his thought and in his works" (ibid., 2:421). Cervantes' affection for Ariosto, too, like his obvious familiarity with the romances of chivalry mocked in *Don Quixote*, is more characteristic of the Spain of his youth than the Spain of the beginning of the seventeenth century, when, already in his fifties, he wrote his great novel (Chevalier 1966, 489–91).

However out of place Cervantes may have felt himself, *Don Quixote* offers plenty of evidence that he understood the Spain of 1605 very well indeed. "*Don Quixote*, this 'universal' book, this 'eternal' book," writes Pierre Vilar,

> is first and foremost a Spanish book of 1605. It acquires its full meaning only if it is placed in its historical context. . . . It has often been said that it would be idle to search in Cervantes for an interpretation of the "decadence" of his country, "because he could not have foreseen it." To say this is to have a singular disregard for chronology. For . . . it is surely between 1598 and 1620 . . . that we must situate the decisive crisis of Spanish power, and, much more surely still, the first great crisis of Spanish self-confidence. (1956, 3)

43

It is easy to see now, with the benefit of hindsight, that the causes of Spain's decline must be sought well back in the sixteenth century and to some extent even before. But an awareness that something had gone terribly wrong seems to have become widespread only toward the end of the century. "As long as Philip II lived," J. H. Elliott observes,

the Castilians had been carried along, half proud, half reluctant, in the wake of a great imperial ideal. There had been great defeats but there had also been great victories, as if to confirm that while God's children had sinned grievously, yet at the end He had not forgotten them. And then, suddenly, everything changed. In 1598 the king died. In 1599 Castile and Andalusia were ravaged by a terrible plague. The years around 1600 were terrible years of famine and labour shortage and spiralling food prices. (1963, 182–83)

There was no shortage of proposals for curing the ills that afflicted Spain. Elliott points out in a superb essay that "early seventeenth-century Spain ... felt itself increasingly threatened and disoriented as two currents of reform competed for attention—one pressing for a return to the ancient ways, the other for innovating change" (1977, 57). He adds that "it would be ... misleading to postulate a clear-cut division between traditionalists and innovators in early seventeenth-century Spain. The currents, in fact, were hopelessly mixed. Proponents of innovating economic remedies also tended to think in terms of collective guilt and moral regeneration" (ibid., 58).

Analyses of the problems of Spain and proposals for their solution were offered by the *arbitristas*. The word has no real equivalent in modern English, though "schemer" comes close. Elliott observes that "an almost exact contemporary

English equivalent of [*arbitrios* and *arbitristas*] exists in 'projects' and 'projectors', even to the pejorative overtones which they both acquired.... Sometimes a crook and more frequently a crank, [the arbitrista] might recommend anything from a secret alchemical formula infallibly guaranteed to refill the king's depleted coffers, to the most grandiose political and military projects" (ibid., 43). Don Quixote's plan to counter the threat of a Turkish invasion by organizing a company of knights-errant (2.1.43), a plan he calls "el más fácil, el más justo y el más mañero y breve que puede caber en pensamiento de arbitrante alguno" (the easiest, most just, most practical and quickest that any projector could imagine) is only a little more absurd than some of the arbitrios proposed in all seriousness by Cervantes' contemporaries.

Not all of the arbitristas were crackpots. Some of them diagnosed the problems of Spain in ways that still command the respect of economic historians. The most important is perhaps Martín González de Cellorigo, an official in the chancery of Valladolid, whose *Memorial de la politica necesaria y util restauracion à la republica de España* was published in Valladolid in 1600. González de Cellorigo insists that Spain resembles nothing so much as a society of the bewitched, living outside the natural order of things, "una republica de hombres encantados, que vivan fuera del orden natural" (folio 25 verso). The reason is that Spaniards refuse to devote themselves to productive labor:

Lo que mas ha distraydo à los nuestros de la legitima ocupacion, que tanto importa à esta republica, ha sido poner tanto la honra y la authoridad en el huyr del trabajo: estimando en poco à los que siguen la agricultura, los tratos, los comercios, y todo qualquier genero de manifactura: contra toda buena politica.... Nues-

tros Españoles son todos affectadores de honra, y ...
quieren mas su estimacion, que quantos thesoros se les
pueden dar: que se puede estimar de semejantes consti-
tuciones: sino que todos desamparen los tratos, ò que
por lo menos en llegando a una mediana ganancia los
dexen: por dexar à sus hijos occasion para adelante, de
yr adquiriendo nobleza, por medio de la renta. (folio 25
recto and verso)

(What has most turned our people away from the legiti-
mate occupations that are so important to the nation is
that they have assigned so much honor and authority to
fleeing from work and have shown little esteem for
those who practice agriculture, trade, commerce, and
any sort of manufacturing: in defiance of all good policy.... We Spaniards are all concerned with honor,
and prefer reputation to any treasures that may be given
us. What can be expected from such a state of things?
Only that everyone neglects productive work, or at least
gives it up as soon as he has amassed a modest fortune,
leaving his children to acquire nobility by living on what
they have inherited.)

Most of the arbitristas, unlike González de Cellorigo, stub-
bornly refused to reveal the solutions they proposed for
Spain's difficulties until they could gain the ear of the proper
authorities, for fear that the credit—and the reward—for
their schemes would go to someone else. Don Quixote similarly resists the priest's urging that he divulge his plan for
saving Spain from the threat of Turkish invasion:

No querría—dijo don Quijote—que le dijese yo aquí
agora, y amaneciese mañana en los oídos de los señores
consejeros, y se llevase otro las gracias y el premio de mi
trabajo. (2.1.43)

("I should not like to reveal it here and now," said Don Quixote, "only to have it reach the ears of the gentlemen of the Council tomorrow morning and to see someone else receive the thanks and the reward for my labor.")

Though many of the works of the arbitristas remain unpublished today, many others were published in the seventeenth century. That Cervantes was familiar with some of them is clear. As Jean-Pierre Vilar has noted (1967), Don Quixote's language often recalls that of the arbitristas. In part 1, chapter 1, when Don Quixote first plans to become a knight-errant, Cervantes tells us that he does so "así para el aumento de su honra como para el servicio de su república ... deshaciendo todo género de agravio" (1.1.74–75) (as much in order to increase his own honor as to serve his nation [by] righting every kind of wrong). Captain Tomás de Cardona of Seville presented his great scheme to protect gold and silver in very similar terms: "Desde el año de 1600, sin perdonar a trabajos y desvelos increibles, fui persiguiendo con mi intento y summo deseo del bien publico" (Since the year 1600, at the cost of unimaginable labors and anxieties, I have continued to pursue my intent and my devotion to the public good). And again, in words that bring to mind Don Quixote's arguments with his niece and his housekeeper, to say nothing of the priest and the barber, Cardona insists that "no desisti de mi intento ... dando por bien empleado mis desvelos, y las reprehensiones de deudos y amigos, y aun domesticas, por averme tanto entregado a esta causa publica" (quoted in Jean-Pierre Vilar 1967, 125) (I have not abandoned my purpose, considering my efforts well spent despite the rebukes of relatives and friends, and even of maidservants, for having dedicated myself so unsparingly to the public good). Another arbitrista, Juan Carreño de Miranda, offered to help the King "deshazer agravios, satisfazer quexas, hazer justicia con despacho recto y breve, remediar necesidades justas, quitar las ocasiones de las discordias, zizañas y pleytos injustos" in order to help "los pobres labradores, los oficiales aflixidos, donzellas, viudas, huerfanos" and protect them from "tiranias, agravios, y pleytos injustos, hambres, frios, prisiones y trabajos que no se pueden sufrir" (redress grievances, satisfy demands, provide for just needs, and remove the causes of disputes and unjustified lawsuits in order to help poor peasants, needy officials, damsels, widows, and orphans and protect them from tyrannies, insults, unjustified lawsuits, hunger, cold, and unbearable sufferings) (ibid., 125).

While the causes of Spain's economic difficulties pointed out by the more perceptive arbitristas may not have been widely recognized, the difficulties themselves must have been obvious to everyone. Much of Castile had become a region of depopulated villages and abandoned farms as their former residents sought a better life in the cities; in other parts of the kingdom the pressure of a growing population had resulted in not only the cultivation of marginal fields and diminishing per capita harvests but also in increasing competition for the available land (Weisser 1973). Sancho's readiness to accompany Don Quixote is not due solely to his ignorance and credulity but reflects a rational awareness of a disastrous economic situation that may well have seemed to offer him no other means of escape.

Don Quixote's economic situation, while far less desperate than his squire's, is not wholly different. "The *hidalgos*," as Antonio Domínguez Ortiz notes, "made up the proletariat of the nobility. They lived off small rents from modest rural domains, and sometimes even worked with their hands. More than one found himself reduced to the proud mendicancy satirized in the literature of the age" (1971, 113). In the opening pages of part 1, Cervantes' detailed account of Don Quixote's income and how he spends it is less likely to have moved his contemporaries to compassion than to scorn for a traditional butt of satire.

Don Quixote belongs to a class both strongly and adversely affected by the modernization of Spanish society in the six-teenth century. The rise of a strong centralized monarchy and the transformation of warfare brought about by the in-vention of firearms had left the hidalgos with no real func-tion, as Don Quixote himself knows only too well. He de-clares that nowadays most knights are more accustomed to wear brocade, damask and other rich fabrics than coats of mail, "los más de los caballeros que agora se usan, antes les crujen los damascos, los brocados y otras ricas telas de que se visten, que la malla con que se arman" (2.1.48). The nostalgia Don Quixote feels for the age of knight-errantry—an age, of course, that he could never have known at first hand—is natural in, and perhaps typical of, a member of a class that had been left with no outlet for its energies (Lloréns 1974).

Don Quixote's situation as a member of this class goes a long way toward explaining the powerful attraction exercised upon him by the romances of chivalry. Maxime Chevalier suggests that the romances were bought and read primarily by members of the nobility, who found in them an idealized portrait of the society in which they themselves lived, or rather would have liked to live:

> Aristocratic readers must have enjoyed the pure and unreal world of the books of chivalry, a world that has no place for the merchant, where money is of no impor-tance, where the city, the site of the economic activities of the bourgeoisie, never appears. (1976, 98)

> Knights found in the imaginary adventures they read about in the romances a compensation for a way of life that was already subject to regulation and would soon be forced to surrender completely. (ibid., 100)

49

The popularity of *Orlando furioso* in the court circles to which it was originally addressed undoubtedly had similar causes. Emilio Bigi remarks that the first version of Ariosto's poem, published in 1516, reveals "an acute and lucid awareness of the crisis of humanistic and Christian ethical values, as well as a realistic conviction of the difficulty of applying them in the real world, especially the contemporary world dominated by blind Fortune and by irrational passions" (1982, 1:33). The additional episodes published posthumously in 1545 and now known as the *Cinque canti* are quite different in both spirit and style. Just when they were written is uncertain; Ariosto may have begun work on them as early as 1519 and then put them aside for several years (Brand 1974, 172). He did not include them in the definitive edition of 1532, for which he wrote four new episodes, including the story of Olimpia, which occupies the greater part of cantos 9 through 11. These new additions return to the tone of the first version; in them, as Bigi notes, we find neither "the bitter and polemical pessimism" that pervades the *Cinque canti*, nor "an unconditional faith in humanistic and Christian values," but a return, "on a rather different plane, to the tension between the ideal and the real that had characterized the first version of *Orlando furioso*" (1982, 1:35).

Ariosto often calls attention to the similarity between the politically purposeless feats accomplished by his knights and the equally purposeless activities of his contemporaries who were denied any effective political role in a war-torn Italy dominated by foreign powers. His characters disregard all other obligations in the frenetic pursuit of their own self-interest. Orlando himself ignores his duty as a soldier in order to go in search of Angelica. Rinaldo, sent to Britain by Charlemagne to recruit fresh troops to relieve the siege of

Paris, goes wandering off in search of adventures as soon as he arrives in Scotland:

> Senza scudiero e senza compagnia
> va il cavallier per quella selva immensa,
> facendo or una et or un'altra via,
> dove piú aver strane aventure pensa. (4.54.1–4)

(Without a squire or any other company, he travels through that immense forest, taking now one path and now another, in search of new adventures.)

Ariosto's contemporaries could hardly have failed to notice the similarity to their own rulers, who plotted and fought against each other instead of uniting against France and Spain, which were quarreling over the division of their homeland. The readiness of some Italian princes and city-states to settle their differences by enlisting the support of foreign powers is reflected in Olimpia's account of her unsuccessful attempts to free Bireno from Cimosco, who has taken him prisoner:

> Sei castella ebbi in Fiandra, e l'ho vendute:
> e 'l poco o 'l molto prezzo ch'io n'ho tratto, parte,
> tentando per persone astute
> i guardiani corrumpere, ho distratto;
> e parte, per far muovere alli danni
> di quell'empio or gl'Inglesi, or gli Alamanni.
> (9.48.3–8)

(I had six castles in Flanders, and I sold them all, and however little or much I got for them I spent, part of it to pay people to bribe his guards, and part of it to persuade the English and the Germans to wage war against that scoundrel.)

Sometimes the accusation is even more direct, as in Ariosto's famous apostrophe to Italy:

> O d'ogni vizio fetida sentina,
> dormi, Italia imbriaca, e non ti pesa
> ch'ora di questa gente, ora di quella
> che già serva ti fu, sei fatta ancella? (17.76.5–8)

(And you, Italy, fetid sink of every vice, are you sleeping in a drunken stupor? Doesn't it trouble you that you are now subject to this nation, now to that, which were once your slaves?)

Nothing in *Don Quixote* is comparable to such passages. It is understandable that some scholars have denied that Cervantes' novel makes any sort of political point. Erich Auerbach, for instance, asserts that Don Quixote's idealism

> is not based on an understanding of actual conditions in this world. Don Quixote does have such an understanding but it deserts him as soon as the idealism of his idée fixe takes hold of him. Everything he does in that state is completely senseless and so incompatible with the existing world that it produces only comic confusion there. It not only has no chance of success, it actually has no point of contact with reality; it expends itself in a vacuum. (1953b, 344)

No doubt Auerbach is right in stressing that Don Quixote's vision of the revival of knight-errantry has nothing to do with the real problems of Spain. But it is one thing to say that Don Quixote does not act from political motives and quite another to imply, as Auerbach does, that Cervantes' novel is unconcerned with the political issues of the time. Cervantes' point may be precisely that Don Quixote's approach to the problems confronting Spain at the beginning of the seventeenth century has as little to do with contemporary reality, and therefore as little chance of success, as the solutions proposed by those who wanted to return to a past that had ceased to exist and that could not possibly be revived.

P. E. Russell rightly emphasizes that "like Ariosto before him, [Cervantes'] mockery of the chivalry books is mingled with understanding of and respect for the ideas that they sought to express" (1985, 108). This shared attitude toward chivalry and the uses that earlier writers had made of it must have helped to inspire Cervantes' admiration for *Orlando furioso*. But though Cervantes shared Don Quixote's respect for chivalric ideals, he did not share his nostalgia for the age of chivalry. Vicente Lloréns has noted the opposition between Cervantes' attitude and that of his great rival Lope de Vega, who, in a period of absolute monarchy, celebrated the restoration of the heroic and chivalresque ideals of the Middle Ages. In Lloréns' view, what Cervantes satirizes in the figure of Don Quixote is neither his self-appointed role as arbitrista nor the nature of the remedy he proposes. It is simply that the remedy offers no hope of a cure: "If Cervantes was opposed to the restoration of the past, it is certainly not because he thought that the heroic ideal—the ideal of his youth—was inadequate. . . . But it belonged to the past and any attempt to restore it in the present could lead only to failure" (1967, 222).

José Antonio Maravall offers a fuller statement of the same view, arguing that Cervantes' novel reflects "a twofold refusal to conform": that of Don Quixote with respect to the world that surrounds him, and that of Cervantes with respect to the pseudoutopian programs of restoration proposed by some of his contemporaries (1976, 70). Like Lloréns, Maravall contends that Cervantes' refusal to accept the premises of

Spanish society in his time is a rejection not of the need for reform but of the specific kind of irrational reform reflected in Don Quixote's attempt to turn back the clock by reviving the institution of knight-errantry (ibid., 80).

Those who seek the restoration of Spain by exalting a chivalresque and pastoral ideal irrelevant to contemporary conditions are guilty of the same error as Don Quixote. Cervantes rejects their unjustified optimism just as he rejects the romances of chivalry, because they make virtue look easy and thus lull their readers into a complacency that has no basis in fact.

CHAPTER IV

Imitation in Ariosto and Cervantes

Some books proclaim their relationship to others. They demand that we read them as new answers to old questions, ones posed, perhaps centuries before, in other books. Both *Don Quixote* and *Orlando furioso* are books of this kind.

Orlando furioso is full of allusions to earlier writers: Dante, Virgil, and Ovid, to name only the most important. And all three of Ariosto's models themselves refer to—and reshape—earlier works. The *Aeneid* constantly echoes the Homeric poems, though Virgil's conception of epic is very different from Homer's, just as Dante's Christianity transforms his borrowings from Virgil. The Renaissance, in rediscovering the classics, rediscovered a kind of intertextuality that had been practiced by the ancient writers themselves. Renaissance writers rediscovered the art of imitation.

In the tenth book of his *Institutiones*, the most influential of all treatises on rhetoric, Quintilian warns against the notion that an imitation is a mere copy of the original. On the contrary, "its function is rather to rival and vie with the original in the expression of the same meaning" (quoted in English in Cave 1979, 36). The first writer to distinguish the kind of imitation that seeks to surpass the original from imitation in general seems to have been Erasmus.

In his *Ciceronianus*, Erasmus distinguishes imitation (*imitatio*) from emulation (*aemulatio*). In both imitatio and aemulatio the essential requirement is that the poet must transform the materials he borrows: mere copying is not true imitation.

According to Erasmus, the difference between the two is that "imitation aims at similarity; emulation, at victory. Thus, if you take all of Cicero and him alone for your model, you should not only reproduce him but also defeat him. He must not be just passed by, but rather left behind." Erasmus returns to the distinction toward the end of his dialogue. The imitator, he declares, "desires to say not so much the same things as similar ones—in fact sometimes not even similar, but rather equal things. But the emulator strives to speak better, if he can" (quoted in English in Pigman 1980, 24, 25).

The relationship between two texts that Erasmus calls aemulatio corresponds roughly to the fourth of the five types studied by Gérard Genette in his *Palimpsestes*. Genette calls this relationship hypertextuality and defines it as the relationship between a text B, which he calls the hypertext, and an earlier text A, which he calls the hypotext. Virgil's *Aeneid* and Joyce's *Ulysses* are hypertexts of the same hypotext, the *Odyssey* (1982, 11–12). *Orlando furioso* is a hypertext of several different hypotexts, the most important of which are Boiardo's *Orlando innamorato*, Virgil's *Aeneid* and Dante's *Divine Comedy*.

Ariosto's relationship to his models is often the competitive kind that Erasmus calls aemulatio, a point frequently stressed in the sixteenth-century commentaries. Dolce (1570), for example, insists that Ariosto's account in canto 6 of Astolfo transformed into a myrtle surpasses his model Virgil's description of Aeneas's encounter with the shade of Polydorus in book 3 of the *Aeneid*: "La inventione di Astolfo trasformato in Mirto, è tolta da Polidoro di Virgilio. Ma è molto piú quello che l'Ariosto vi aggiunge. Et forse chi ben considera le due comparationi, & con qual vaghezza questa fintione è detta dal nostro poeta, potrà credere, che egli in tal luogo habbia Virgilio superato."

56

The emulator wants not only to surpass his model but also to make his reader conscious that he has done so. For this reason he makes no attempt to hide the relationship between his own text and the text he has chosen as a model, but tries instead to call attention to it. Ariosto's title *Orlando furioso* evokes both its most famous and most immediate predecessor, Boiardo's *Orlando innamorato*, and a more remote and more illustrious one, Seneca's tragedy *Hercules furens*. The title *Orlando furioso*, like the opening pages of the book itself, gives the reader a foretaste of the kind of experience that awaits him. It alerts him to the relationship between the book he is just beginning and other books that he has already read, as the words "once upon a time" tell a child that he is about to enter the exciting but comfortingly familiar world of the fairy tale. Alastair Fowler has noted that "the generic markers that cluster at the beginning of a text have a strategic role in guiding the reader. They help to establish, as soon as possible, an appropriate mental 'set' that allows the work's generic codes to be read. One might call them the key words of the code, although they may serve this purpose at an unconscious level, or at least beneath the level of attention" (1982, 88). But while the generic markers may operate beneath the level of the reader's attention, there is every reason to suppose that the poets who used them were perfectly aware of what they were doing. Fowler notes that "Renaissance theorists gave close attention to the rhetorical 'parts' of an epic fiction that came before the narrative itself—such as the *principium*, or indication of the action's scope; the *invocatio*; the *exordium*, setting the opening scene; and the *ianua narrandi* or opening of the action itself" (ibid., 102).

The first lines of Ariosto's poem echo Virgil's "Arma virumque cano," though with the important difference that Ariosto proposes to sing not just of men and arms but of women too: "Le donne, i cavallier, l'arme, gli amori, / le cortesie, l'audaci imprese io canto," which Barbara Reynolds renders "Of ladies, cavaliers, of love and war, / Of courtesies and of brave deeds I sing."

The first stanza establishes Ariosto's proud claim that his poem belongs to the tradition of Virgilian epic. The claim— not wholly serious, of course, but not just a joke either—is embodied both in the words he uses and in the way they are joined together. The whole stanza consists of a single beautifully articulated complex sentence that demonstrates Ariosto's mastery of the Virgilian style. The impression of self-conscious mastery established in the first stanza of *Orlando furioso* is, however, undercut by Ariosto's revelation in the very next stanza that his love for his lady has come close to driving him as mad as Orlando himself. The same pattern will recur throughout the poem. The bits of sententious advice that often serve to introduce a new canto are sometimes followed immediately by the poet's confession that he has not been able to practice what he preaches. Ariosto speaks sometimes as the traditional epic poet who serves as the spokesman for a community and for an established code of values, sometimes as an all too fallible individual whose ability to see beyond the illusory surface of events and to govern his own life rationally is no greater than that of his characters.

Ariosto's many echoes of earlier poets, especially Dante (Segre 1966) and Virgil, keep the reader aware that *Orlando furioso* belongs to a rich and varied tradition. This awareness creates a bond between the poet and his audience. The comic effect of Ruggiero's encounter with Astolfo on Alcina's island in canto 6 depends in part on the reader's recognizing it as a variation of one of the most dramatic scenes in the *Divine Comedy*, Dante's meeting with Pier della Vigna in canto 13 of the *Inferno*. Ruggiero finds Astolfo transformed into a myrtle just as Dante encounters Pier della Vigna transformed into a great thornbush. Dante's text in turn evokes Aeneas' meeting with the shade of Polydorus who, like Astolfo, appears transformed into a myrtle in book 3 of the *Aeneid*.

Many of Ariosto's subtlest and most complex effects depend, like this one, on the reader's intimate familiarity with a few canonical texts. The wood through which Angelica flees from her pursuers in canto 1 is described by a series of terms that bring it steadily closer to Dante's "selva oscura," the dark wood mentioned in the second line of the *Inferno*. First called a "bosco" in stanza 10, it becomes a "foresta" and then "l'alta selva fiera" in stanza 13, and finally becomes "selve spaventose e scure" in stanza 33. Here both the word "scure" and the rhyme with "paure" recall Dante's "selva oscura ... che nel pensier rinova la paura," the dark wood of *Inferno* 1.2–6, so terrifying that even the thought of it fills the heart with fear. The fullest evocation of Dante's lines is not reached until 2.68.4–5, where Ariosto tells us that Ruggiero "ritrovossi in una selva oscura." Here "selva" again rimes with "paura" as it does in Dante and the verb "ritrovossi" recalls the familiar opening lines of the *Inferno*: "Nel mezzo del cammin di nostra vita / mi ritrovai per una selva oscura" (in the middle of the journey of our life I found myself in a dark wood).

Ariosto's evocation of Dante's "selva oscura" serves first of all as a generic marker to remind the reader that Ariosto's poem belongs in some sense to the same class as Dante's, despite the enormous differences in tone and subject matter. It serves also as a hint that the wood through which Angelica pursues her headlong course, like the other wood in which Ruggiero finds himself, is the wood of human life on earth. Most of all, it points to the ways in which both Angelica's frenetic flight and Ruggiero's journey in search of adventure are at once like and unlike the situation of Dante's traveler, for whom the straight way was lost, "la diritta via era smarrita" (*Inferno* 1.3).

Ariosto's use of quotations from and allusions to Latin and vernacular models in order to juxtapose radically different poetic worlds was not available to Cervantes. Ariosto could use the generic markers of epic both to establish the kind of poem he was writing and also to mark the distance between his own work and that of his predecessors: *Orlando furioso* is both a successor to Virgil's epic and an anti-*Aeneid*. Cervantes could not rely on such generic markers because the novel in his day had, and to a large extent still has, no established formal conventions of its own.

Cervantes could not follow Ariosto's example for still another reason: the Spanish literary tradition available to him offered no classic texts comparable to the Italian ones that Ariosto could draw upon. Spain had had no Dante, no Petrarch or Boccaccio. Garcilaso had come closer than any other Spanish writer to achieving the stature of the *tre corone* of Florence, thanks in part to the annotated editions by Francisco Sánchez de las Brozas (1575, enlarged 1577) and Fernando de Herrera (1580). Echoes of Garcilaso resound throughout Cervantes' works, not least in *Don Quixote*. But although undoubtedly present, these echoes are far more fleeting and less apt to catch the reader's attention than the extended similes that reveal Ariosto's debt to Virgil and Dante.

Nor could Cervantes use Latin models as Ariosto uses Virgil and Ovid. If Ariosto presents himself in the opening stanzas of *Orlando furioso* as both a follower and a rival of Virgil, Cervantes presents himself in the prologue to part 1 of *Don Quixote* as a writer so unskilled that he does not even know how to compose a proper introduction to his own work. Other parents, he tells us, are blind to their children's faults and may even think that the faults are virtues:

> Pero yo, que, aunque parezco padre, soy padrastro de don Quijote, no quiero irme con la corriente del uso, ni suplicarte casi con las lágrimas en los ojos, como otros hacen, lector carísimo, que perdones o disimules las faltas que en este mi hijo vieres, y ni eres su pariente ni su amigo, y tienes tu alma en tu cuerpo y tu libre albedrío como el más pintado, y estás en tu casa, donde eres señor della, como el rey de sus alcabalas, y sabes lo que comúnmente se dice, que debajo de mi manto, al rey mato. (50–51)

> (But, though I may seem to be Don Quixote's father, I am really his stepfather, and I have no intention of following the fashion and begging you, dearest reader, almost with tears in my eyes, as others do, to pardon or overlook whatever flaws you see in this child of mine, for you are neither a relative nor a friend of his, and your soul is your own and your will as free as any other man's and you are master in your house as the king is of his revenues, and you know the saying "a man's home is his castle" [literally, "beneath my cloak I kill the king"].)

The confident mastery of syntax and subject matter that marks Ariosto's opening stanzas contrasts sharply with Cervantes' syntactic looseness in this passage and his failure—surely deliberate—to maintain either a coherent logical structure or a consistent level of style.

A few lines further on Cervantes reveals his reluctance to place before the public a tale dry as a bone, lacking invention, deficient in style, poor in conceits and quite without learning and doctrine, "una leyenda seca como un esparto, ajena de invención, menguada de estilo, pobre de concetos y falta de toda erudición y doctrina" (52). An authorial role of this kind offers little scope for the virtuoso demonstrations of craftsmanship that turn up everywhere in *Orlando furioso*.

There are indeed classical allusions in *Don Quixote*, but they are of an entirely different kind from the echoes of Virgil, Ovid, and Dante in which Ariosto delights. The most obvious is perhaps Don Quixote's descent into the Cave of Montesinos, which recalls Aeneas' descent into the underworld. Peter Dunn has suggested that the country house of the Duke and Duchess "powerfully recalls the island of Circe," and he compares Don Quixote's discovery that his fame has preceded him because his hosts have read part 1 to Aeneas' experience when Dido welcomes him to Carthage, which in turn recalls Odysseus' reception by the Phaeacians after his shipwreck (1972, 5). Although these resemblances must have been obvious to many of Cervantes' contemporaries, they do not signal their relationship to another text by appropriating its words as do many of Ariosto's evocations of Dante, or this image drawn from Ovid's *Heroides* to highlight the resemblance between Olimpia, abandoned by Bireno, and Ariadne, mourning the departure of Theseus from Naxos:

> Or si ferma s'un sasso, e guarda il mare;
> né men d'un vero sasso, un sasso pare. (10.34.7–8)

which Barbara Reynolds wonderfully renders "Olimpia gazes seawards, like a stock, / Standing so still, a rock upon a rock." In passages like these, Ariosto incorporates an earlier text into his own in order to reveal the kinship between his work and that of his illustrious predecessors and also to call attention to the differences that separate his work from theirs.

Cervantes rarely shapes episodes, as Ariosto does, to make them recall similar—often, of course, only superficially similar—episodes in the writings of his predecessors. No episode in *Don Quixote* recalls a classical model as directly as Ariosto's Olimpia recalls Dido abandoned by Aeneas, and, even more directly, Ariadne abandoned by Theseus. A reader familiar with the *Aeneid* might well think Dorotea reminiscent of Dido. She has managed her father's farm efficiently, as Dido has managed the kingdom she inherited from her murdered husband. Like Dido, too, Dorotea insists, though with far better cause, that the man who abandoned her is her husband and, again like Dido, she has some harsh things to say about him. There, however, the resemblance ends. Dorotea is not driven mad by rage and frustration like Dido. Instead, she very sensibly sets out in pursuit of Don Fernando in order to try to persuade him to accept her as his wife. Neither Dorotea herself nor the narrator explicitly says anything linking her to Dido; nothing in Cervantes' story evokes Virgil in the way that Ariosto's image of Olimpia on a rock, as motionless and devoid of feeling as the rock itself, evokes Ovid's Ariadne.

Elsewhere, however, Cervantes does refer to Dido. Or rather—and this is the crucial difference between his treatment and Ariosto's—he makes Don Quixote himself refer to her in the wonderful scene when Doña Rodríguez comes to his bedroom in the middle of the night to ask him to help her find the young man who has seduced her daughter:

> —¿Estamos seguras, señor caballero? Porque no tengo a muy honesta señal haberse vuestra merced levantado de su lecho.
>
> —Eso mesmo es bien que yo pregunte, señora—respondió don Quijote—; y así, pregunto si estaré yo seguro de ser acometido y forzado.

—¿De quién o a quién pedís, señor caballero, esa seguridad?—respondió la dueña.

—A vos y de vos la pido—respondió don Quijote—; porque ni yo soy de mármol ni vos de bronce, ni ahora son las diez del día, sino media noche, y aun un poco más, según imagino, y en una estancia más cerrada y secreta que lo debió de ser la cueva donde el traidor y atrevido Eneas gozó a la hermosa y piadosa Dido. Pero dadme, señora, la mano, que yo no quiero otra seguridad mayor que la de mi continencia y recato, y la que ofrecen esas reverendísimas tocas. (2.48.398–99)

("Am I safe with you, sir knight? For it does not seem to me a good sign that you have gotten out of your bed."

"I might well ask the same thing of you, my lady," replied Don Quixote. "And indeed I do ask whether I am in danger of being assaulted and ravished."

"From whom and with respect to whom do you request that assurance?" replied the lady.

"From you and with respect to you," replied Don Quixote. "For I am not made of marble, nor you of bronze, nor is it now ten o'clock in the morning, but midnight, and I think even a little past, and in a room as secluded and secret as the cave where the treacherous and bold Aeneas possessed the fair and pious Dido. But give me your hand, my lady, for I do not need any protection other than my own continence and sense of propriety and those widow's weeds you wear.")

Don Quixote calls Dido pious, a term Virgil applies repeatedly to Aeneas, and one quite inappropriate to Dido. Virgil stresses rather the impiety of her behavior, which constitutes a breach of faith toward her dead husband and endangers the security of her kingdom, whose needs no longer engage her attention. Don Quixote fears that Doña Rodríguez may attempt to ravish him in a comic reversal of roles that is of course absent in Virgil. His reference to "el traidor y atrevido Eneas" reveals that, like Dido, he is unwilling to accept Aeneas' claim that he has no choice but to leave Carthage and proceed to Italy: "Italiam non sponte sequor" (*Aeneid* 4.361). Don Quixote's conception of chivalry does not allow for the possibility that the knight's devotion to his mission may conflict with his devotion to his lady.

Dido is mentioned again near the end of part 2. As Don Quixote and Sancho are returning home to their village after Don Quixote's defeat by the Knight of the White Moon, they see in the dining room of an inn some painted tapestries depicting Helen of Troy and Dido. The sight of the tapestries prompts Sancho to remark that soon every inn and tavern will be adorned with paintings of his master's adventures, "antes de mucho tiempo no ha de haber bodegón, venta ni mesón, o tienda de barbero, donde no ande pintada la historia de nuestras hazañas" (2.71.574). The scene recalls Aeneas' discovery of scenes from his own life on the walls of the temple in Carthage; Sancho's reference to Don Quixote's future fame is a transparent attempt to help his master shake off his mood of black despondency as Aeneas takes heart— "sunt lacrimae rerum et mentem mortalia tangunt" (1.462)— from the discovery that his misfortunes can touch men's hearts even in distant Carthage. Sancho, of course, knows nothing of this, and Don Quixote, who surely does, is not to be comforted so easily. He does not compare his situation to that of Aeneas but limits himself to commenting on the poor quality of the paintings. Don Quixote's failure to notice the parallel and to take heart from it is a clear indication that his morale is at its lowest point.

Elsewhere, Don Quixote refers to Aeneas in ways that reveal a certain hostility. He stresses that Virgil has not depicted Aeneas as he was but as he ought to have been so that he might serve as an example to future generations (1.25.303). He makes the same point again when he tells Sancho and Sansón Carrasco that "no fue tan piadoso Eneas como Virgilio le pinta" (2.3.61), echoing Ariosto's "Non sí pietoso Enea, né forte Achille / fu, come è fama, né sí fiero Ettorre" (35.25.1–2) (Aeneas was not so pious, nor Achilles so strong, as people say, nor was Hector so fierce). Cervantes slyly makes Don Quixote suggest that books are not always to be trusted, thus undercutting his own faith in the truthfulness of the romances of chivalry, and hence their usefulness as guides to conduct.

The bond between poet and reader that Ariosto creates by repeated allusions to other familiar books does not extend to his characters. Ariosto seldom makes his characters allude to other literary works. One of the few times he does so is the occasion when Bradamante, despairing because Ruggiero has failed to return at the appointed time, wonders whether the horses of the sun have become lame and thinks every day longer than the one on which Joshua stopped the sun and every night longer than the one Jupiter extended in order to prolong his pleasure with Alcmena (32.11). But this passage is exceptional. Ruggiero and Astolfo are unaware that their meeting on Alcina's island in canto 6 evokes Dante's meeting with Pier della Vigna in canto 13 of the *Inferno*, just as Olimpia is unaware that her impassioned outburst on being abandoned by Bireno echoes that of Ariadne in Ovid's *Heroides*. None of Ariosto's characters cares anything about literature. The book of cures and counterspells that Logistilla gives Astolfo serves merely as a handy reference work, thanks to its chapter headings and analytical index (15.14.1–4). Neither Astolfo nor any of the other characters ever reads a book for pleasure.

None of Ariosto's characters try to reshape their lives to make them more like the fictional lives they have read about, as Don Quixote and many of the other characters in Cervantes' novel do. Dorotea can play the role of Princess Micomicona so well because she is familiar with romances of chivalry; as Márquez Villanueva has noted (1975, 26), she is less than candid when she says that she found relief from the cares of managing her father's farm in reading devotional books (1.28.349). The adventures that the Duke and Duchess stage for Don Quixote and Sancho reveal that they and other members of their court—Altisidora, for example, or the majordomo—are similarly at home in the world of the romances of chivalry. Even Sancho, unable to read or write and proud of it, is steeped in the proverbs and folktales that form the literary heritage of the unlettered. He remembers things he has heard in sermons and absorbs his master's teaching so well that he can deceive him by making him believe that evil enchanters have transformed Dulcinea into the peasant woman he meets in part 2, chapter 10. All of these characters, and many others, are not merely readers or listeners, but creators of literature.

In general, Ariosto's characters act with the serene self-confidence of their distant prototypes in the *Chanson de Roland*, for whom, as Erich Auerbach observes, "nothing of fundamental significance is problematic" (1953b, 110). But the world of *Orlando furioso* is no longer the aristocratic feudal world of medieval French epic. In the epic, as Auerbach notes, the characters "always perform a historico-political function" (ibid., 122). In the courtly romances of Chrétien de Troyes this is no longer true:

> Calogrenant sets out without mission or office; he seeks adventure, that is, perilous encounters by which he can prove his mettle. There is nothing like this in the *chanson de geste*. There a knight who sets off has an office and a place in a politico-historical context. . . . Calogrenant, on the other hand, has no political or historical

task, nor has any other knight of Arthur's court. Here the feudal ethos serves no political function; it serves no practical reality at all; it has become absolute. It no longer has any purpose but that of self-realization. (ibid., 133–34)

The world of *Orlando furioso* is closer to that of Chrétien de Troyes than to that of the *Chanson de Roland*. Orlando, Ruggiero, and the other principal characters are engaged in a war between Christians and infidels, just as in the *Chanson de Roland*, but the war occupies a much less central position in Ariosto's poem. It is all but forgotten for long stretches, not only by the narrator and the reader, but also by the characters themselves. Ariosto's world is nevertheless quite different from Chrétien's, for Ariosto's characters are not engaged in a perilous voyage of self-discovery, nor are they dedicated to the service of an ethical ideal. They simply want to satisfy their own desires, often—though not always—erotic ones.

Because Ariosto's characters owe no allegiance to anything except the satisfaction of their own desires, they seldom feel a need to justify their conduct either to themselves or to anyone else. The pagan knight Ferraù does not stop to consider whether he should help the Christian Rinaldo when the latter asks his help in pursuing Angelica (1.20), nor does Orlando pause to debate whether he should remain with Charlemagne's army or go in search of Angelica after he has dreamed that she is in danger (8.73–78). There are occasional exceptions, like Bradamante's soliloquy weighing the claims of obedience to her mother against those of her love for Ruggiero (44.41–47) or Ruggiero's soliloquy that follows it (44.52–57), but it is worth noting that both are found in the lengthy interpolation extending from canto 44, stanza 35 through canto 46, stanza 72, that Ariosto added to the definitive third edition of *Orlando furioso*. The interpolated material, as scholars have often noted, is quite different in tone from the rest of the poem.

All of Ariosto's principal characters, like Chrétien's or like those of the *Chanson de Roland*, belong to the upper strata of the nobility. The differences in their ranks hardly affect their dealings with one another. Each of them acts as an autonomous being subject only to the law of his or her own desires. Ariosto's characters can scarcely be said to play social roles at all.

By contrast, the world of *Don Quixote* is the world of early modern Europe, in which social roles were quite clearly defined, though it was becoming increasingly easy for individuals to exchange one role for another. The result was the "destabilization of social categories" that Michael McKeon has seen as one cause of the rise of the novel (1987, 131–75). Cervantes takes great care to indicate the precise social and often economic status of his characters. Don Quixote is defined from the outset as an *hidalgo*, a nobleman of the lowest rank and thus different from the *caballeros* who are the protagonists of the romances of chivalry. He is far from well-to-do; the modest meals described in the opening pages of the novel consume three-quarters of his income, and his library of romances has been assembled by selling off part of his land, thus reducing his future income even further. The social and economic position of many of the other characters is presented with the same attention to detail. Marcela and Dorotea are explicitly said to be the daughters of wealthy farmers, *labradores ricos*, as is Leandra; Grisóstomo belongs to the same class, as do Leandra's suitors Eugenio and Anselmo. All of them, and many of the other characters in the book as well, appear in roles other than their socially given ones, usually roles that they have chosen for themselves.

This is obviously true of Don Quixote himself. Almost everyone he meets knows him not as Alonso Quijano, but as

Don Quixote, that is, in the role of knight-errant that he has chosen for himself. The exceptions are his niece and his housekeeper, his neighbors the priest and the barber, Sancho, Sansón Carrasco and the peasant Tomé Cecial who acts as his squire when he takes on the role of the Knight of the Wood, and the other peasant who discovers Don Quixote lying stunned in the road outside his village on his return from his first sally (1.5): eight characters out of the more than five hundred that appear in the novel. Like Don Quixote, many of Cervantes' other characters insist on their claims to the respect of those whom they address not just on the basis of the class to which they belong, but on the basis of their own often wildly idiosyncratic behavior: Marcela's decision to become a shepherdess, Dorotea's to disguise herself as a man and go in search of Don Fernando, and so on.

Ariosto hardly ever assigns one of his characters a formal speech of self-justification like Marcela's address to the shepherds disclaiming responsibility for the death of Grisóstomo (1.14) or the long speech in which Dorotea introduces herself and begins the story of her adventures (1.28). Speeches of this kind are rare in *Orlando furioso* because Ariosto's characters refuse to recognize that society may hold them accountable for their actions. In contrast, Cervantes' characters often reveal a need to explain their conduct to everyone they meet, even when they profess not to care what others think of them. Marcela feels compelled to try to convince the shepherds that she has acted reasonably and justly in refusing to return Grisóstomo's love even though she insists that she needs no sanction for her actions other than the dictates of her own conscience. It is a sign of her self-confidence that she insists on presenting herself before an audience—Grisóstomo's fellow shepherds—that has neither a legal nor, at least in her view, a moral right to judge her. It is moreover, an audience that she surely knows, or ought to know, is hostile to her. There is an obvious conflict between her desire to argue her case and her refusal to say anything that might win the sympathy of her audience.

Don Quixote's self-confidence is not as great as Marcela's. His words and actions often contradict his assertion upon returning from his first sally that "Yo sé quien soy ... y sé que puedo ser ... todos los doce Pares de Francia, y aun todos los nueve de la Fama" (1.5.106) (I know who I am ... and I know that I can be ... all the Twelve Peers of France and even all the Nine Worthies). If he is always ready to explain his motives to others, the reason is, no doubt, that he needs their acceptance to convince himself that he is the knight-errant he claims to be. His dependence on others is demonstrated most clearly by the fact that he first feels sure that he is a knight-errant when the Duke and Duchess treat him as knights are treated in the romances of chivalry: "y aquél fue el primer día en que de todo en todo conoció y creyó ser caballero andante verdadero, y no fantástico, viéndose tratar del mesmo modo que él había leído se trataban los tales caballeros en los pasados siglos" (2.31.274). Like Marcela, Don Quixote depends on others to confirm his sense of who and what he is.

Ariosto's characters hardly ever face the dilemma of choosing between acting as the persons they feel they are or want to be and acting in the way society expects of them. The fact that Cervantes' characters are often faced with dilemmas of this kind makes Don Quixote or Marcela or Dorotea seem closer to us than Orlando or Angelica or Bradamante. Neither Bradamante herself nor anyone else in Ariosto's poem sees anything odd in the fact that she dresses as a man and fights as a knight; she has no need to explain herself as Dorotea does when she first appears dressed as a man (1.28.347). Cervantes' characters reveal a degree of self-consciousness that we should seek in vain in Ariosto's, and this, of course, is one of the reasons why they often seem so much more modern.

Their modernity, however, is of a specific kind, not that of our twentieth century, but that of Cervantes' early modern Europe. Walter R. Davis has noted that

> the action of Elizabethan and Jacobean drama ... often amounts to its hero's self-conscious acting out of a role he has conceived for himself.... The function of the role is to extend the normal possibilities of action for the character involved in it. (1969, 47)

> But the role must be given up at the end of the play, for while it extends the possibilities of action for the hero it also cramps his normally various personality into a strict and narrow channel of purpose. (ibid., 49)

Davis' observation is as true of Spanish literature as of English, as every reader of the *Novelas ejemplares* knows (Hart 1981). Don Quixote's career as a knight-errant, like Sancho's governorship of Barataria, enables him to "extend the normal possibilities of action" by playing a role he could never have attempted if he had remained in his village.

Playing a role is very different from giving free expression to one's own individuality, as Davis' reference to "a strict and narrow channel of purpose" implies. Marthe Robert has observed that "the most radical quixotic act ... is never the accomplishment of some personal ambition, but on the contrary the imitation of an ideal fixed by tradition, indeed by literary convention, and consequently stripped of all originality" (1977, 12). The originality of Don Quixote's career as knight-errant is involuntary, not an expression of his own individual personality but an attempt to escape from it by imitating a model. Don Quixote's imitation is profoundly original, but for him, and to the extent that he is aware of it, this means only that he has failed to achieve his goal.

CHAPTER V

Pastoral Interludes

Cervantes' first published work was a pastoral novel, *La Galatea*. In the prologue he suggests that it is a youthful exercise designed to prepare him for loftier and more significant undertakings, "empresas más altas y de mayor importancia," and thus places himself among the many Renaissance writers—Spenser and Milton are the most obvious English examples—who imitated Virgil by trying their hands at pastoral poetry before attempting more ambitious subjects. *La Galatea*, however, is hardly a juvenile work; Cervantes was thirty-eight when it appeared in 1585. Thirty years later, in the prologue to *Don Quixote*, part 2, he was still promising to write a second part, and he repeated the promise on his deathbed a year later in the dedication of *Persiles y Sigismunda*.

The world of pastoral literature is often evoked in *Don Quixote*. Early in part 1 Don Quixote's niece fears that her uncle will decide to become a shepherd (1.6.118), a prospect she finds as disquieting as his decision to become a knight-errant. Indeed, he does plan to do so toward the end of part 2, when Sansón Carrasco, disguised as the Knight of the White Moon, defeats him and forces him to give up knight-errantry for a year. Several other characters actually do what Don Quixote only thinks of doing: Grisóstomo, Marcela and their friends in part 1, chapter 12, whose decision to adopt a pastoral life anticipates that of Eugenio, Anselmo and *their* friends in part 1, chapter 51. A milder form of the same response to the attractions of the pastoral life may be seen in the "new pastoral Arcady" that Don Quixote visits in part 2,

73

chapter 58. And there are, of course, also plenty of real keepers of flocks, like the shepherds whose sheep Don Quixote mistakes for rival armies (1.18) and the goatherds he meets early in part 1, at the beginning of the first of his pastoral adventures.

The goatherds welcome Don Quixote cordially and invite him and Sancho to share their simple meal. They are puzzled by their guests' conversation about squires and knights-errant, and their perplexity increases when Don Quixote picks up a handful of dried acorns and delivers a long speech in praise of the Golden Age.

In that happy time, he tells the goatherds, the very idea of property was unknown; no one had ever heard the words "mine" and "thine." Nature provided for all man's needs, both physical and emotional. Hearts spoke directly to hearts: "Entonces se decoraban los concetos amorosos del alma simple y sencillamente del mesmo modo y manera que ella los concebía, sin buscar artificioso rodeo de palabras para encarecerlos" (1.11.156). Women feared neither violence nor deceitful persuasion: "Las doncellas y la honestidad andaban ... por dondequiera, sola y señora, sin temor que la ajena desenvoltura y lascivo intento le menoscabasen, y su perdición nacía de su gusto y propria voluntad" (1.11.157) maidens and chastity wandered alone wherever they liked, and their undoing sprang from their own will and pleasure. Don Quixote's use of the word *perdición*, "undoing," in this context shows how different his Golden Age is from that evoked in the chorus that ends the first act of Tasso's pastoral drama *Aminta*. Those who live in Tasso's Golden Age have no moral scruples of any kind. They are free to do whatever they like, confident that "*S'ei piace, ei lice,*" whatever pleases is permissible.

Don Quixote's imagined Golden Age rests on a perfect balance between supply and demand. Since everyone then had everything he wanted, no one had any reason to wish for more, and so everyone lived in harmony with everyone else: "todo era paz entonces, todo amistad, todo concordia" (1.11.156). The pastoral Arcadia created by Marcela, Grisóstomo and their followers is very different. All the young men who follow Grisóstomo's example by becoming shepherds are in love with Marcela and with her alone. The result, as the goatherd Pedro explains to Don Quixote, is that

> si aquí estuviésedes, señor, algún día, veríades resonar estas sierras y estos valles con los lamentos de los desengañados que la siguen. No está muy lejos de aquí un sitio donde hay casi dos docenas de altas hayas, y no hay ninguna que en su lisa corteza no tenga grabado y escrito el nombre de Marcela.... Aquí sospira un pastor, allí se queja otro; acullá se oyen amorosas canciones, acá desesperadas endechas. Cuál hay que pasa todas las horas de la noche sentado al pie de alguna encina o peñasco, y allí, sin plegar los llorosos ojos, embebecido y transportado en sus pensamientos, le halló el sol a la mañana, y cuál hay que, sin dar vado ni tregua a sus sentimientos, en mitad del ardor de la más enfadosa siesta del verano, tendido sobre la ardiente arena, envía sus quejas al piadoso cielo. Y déste y de aquél, y de aquéllos y de éstos, libre y desenfadadamente triunfa la hermosa Marcela. (1.12.166–67)

(If you were to stay here, sir, you would hear the mountains and valleys resound with the laments of her disappointed suitors. Not far from here is a place where there are a couple of dozen tall beeches, and there is not one of them that doesn't have Marcela's name carved and written on its smooth bark.... Here a shepherd sighs, there another moans; in one place are heard love songs, in another songs of lamentation. There is one who spends the whole night seated at the foot of an oak or cliff without closing his tearful eyes and the sun finds him there the next morning in a trance and bereft of his senses. Another, sighing unceasingly, stretches himself out on the burning sand when the summer heat is at its peak and appeals for relief to the merciful heavens. And over this one and that one and over all of them together the beautiful Marcela triumphs free and unconcerned.)

By giving Marcela a large number of competing suitors, Cervantes turns into farce a motif that might have been treated seriously if it had involved a single lover. The suitors' lamentations are revealed as stylized movements of a ritual learned from books, not spontaneous expressions of individual emotion. But the boundary between art and life has been overstepped, and this farcical playacting has had tragic consequences: though neither Pedro nor anyone else says so explicitly, it is clear that Grisóstomo has not just talked about dying for love but has actually killed himself (Herrero 1978, 290–92).

Don Quixote's discourse on the Golden Age stresses the connection between love and property rights. Grisóstomo's suicide raises the same issue. The notion that suicide is a violation of property rights is very old; in Plato's *Phaedo* Socrates asserts that suicide is one of the few acts unlawful under all circumstances, since men are the property of the gods, and property has no right to dispose of itself. The prohibition of suicide became an established part of Christian ethical doctrine. In the *Summa Theologiae* Saint Thomas Aquinas declares that "life is a gift made to man by God, and it is subject to him who is *master of death and life*. Therefore a person who takes his own life sins against God, just as he who kills another's slave injures the slave's master. . . . And God alone has authority to decide about life and death"

(2a2ae 64.5). Grisóstomo's decision to kill himself rests on the mistaken belief that his life is his own and that he is free to dispose of it as he pleases. By killing himself he usurps God's property rights. The love he offers Marcela rests on an implicit analogy between God's right to dispose of his property and the lover's right to dispose of the beloved: Grisóstomo demands exclusive possession of Marcela and kills himself when he cannot get it. Though Marcela rejects the kind of love Grisóstomo offers her, she, too, seems unable to imagine any other kind.

Aquinas asserts also that suicide is always unlawful because "every part belongs to the whole in virtue of what it is. But every man is part of the community, so that he belongs to the community in virtue of what he is. Suicide therefore involves damaging the community." There is no doubt that Grisóstomo's death hurts the village. Pedro reports that Grisóstomo's study of astronomy at the University of Salamanca enabled him to predict which crops would do well in a given year, and that his advice made his father and his father's friends rich. The absolute autonomy Marcela demands damages the community just as Grisóstomo's suicide damages it. If she were to persist in her refusal to marry, and if the other village girls followed her example, as they have followed it by becoming shepherdesses, the community would eventually cease to exist. In this sense, Ambrosio is right to refer to Marcela as a mortal enemy of mankind, "enemiga mortal del linaje humano" (1.13.178). Marcela herself declares that she rejected Grisóstomo's offer of marriage because she had decided that the earth alone should enjoy the fruit of her withdrawal from society and the spoils of her beauty: "cuando . . . me descubrió la bondad de su intención, le dije yo que la mía era vivir en perpetua soledad, y de que sola la tierra gozase el fruto de mi recogimiento y los despojos de mi hermosura" (1.14.187).

The strangeness of the conception of love held by Marcela and Grisóstomo is underscored by the contrast between it and the mutual love of the goatherd Antonio and Olalla, whom Antonio plans to marry. The love celebrated in the song that Antonio sings for Don Quixote immediately following the latter's discourse on the Golden Age (1.11.158–60) is sanctioned by marriage and recognized by the community as essential to its survival. Such a conception of love separates the world of the goatherds from the world of literary shepherds and shepherdesses like Grisóstomo and Marcela just as the name *Olalla*, a rustic form of *Eulalia*, marks the distance between her and the Amaryllises, Phyllidas, and Galateas of more conventional pastorals.

The verses Ambrosio composes as an epitaph for his friend Grisóstomo refer to Marcela as "una esquiva hermosa ingrata" (1.14.189). His phrase identifies her with a familiar literary figure, the *mujer esquiva*, who rejects love and marriage. The *esquiva*'s history has been traced by Melveena McKendrick (1974, 283–85). Several of McKendrick's examples come from Ovid's *Metamorphoses*, among them Anaxarate, alluded to in Garcilaso's *Ode ad florem Gnidi*, whose refusal to accept her lover Iphis causes him to kill himself. Marcela's refusal to accept Grisóstomo's offer of marriage makes her similarly responsible for his death in the eyes of Ambrosio and his friends. Another mujer esquiva, not mentioned by McKendrick, is Ariosto's Angelica, whose memory haunts so many pages of *Don Quixote*. Angelica, of course, finally does fall in love, as do all the other mujeres esquivas who, thanks largely to the influence of Lope de Vega, played so important a role in the Spanish theater just at the time part 1 of *Don Quixote* first appeared in print (ibid., 1974, 143). One reason Ambrosio and the other shepherds refuse to accept Marcela's claim that she is not responsible for Grisóstomo's death is surely that they consider her disdain an attitude not

destined to last forever, as Pedro makes clear when he says
that everyone who knows her is waiting to see which of her
many suitors she will choose: "todos los que la conocemos
estamos esperando en qué ha de parar su altivez y quién ha
de ser el dichoso que ha de venir a domeñar condición tan
terrible y gozar de hermosura tan estremada" (1.12.167). Marcela's "cruelty" to Grisóstomo seems all the more reprehensi-
ble to his friends since they believe that her rejection rests on
a mistaken notion that she will be able to escape the tyranny
of love (Hart and Rendall 1978, 294). Many of Cervantes' first
readers must have expected that Marcela would reappear
later in the novel head over heels in love, as Angelica, after
rejecting Orlando and all her other suitors, finally falls in love
with Medoro, a turn of events that Don Quixote, like some
of Ariosto's sixteenth-century commentators, finds both inex-
plicable and detestable (2.1.51–52).

McKendrick asserts that "none of the playwrights of the
Golden Age sympathizes with his *esquivas* in the way that
Cervantes sympathizes with his Marcela" (1974, 145). Cervantes may have been less sympathetic to Marcela than Mc-
Kendrick believes he was. Sixteenth-century notions of liberty and of woman's role in society were quite different from
our own. Marcela rejects not merely Grisóstomo's offer of
marriage but marriage itself. She insists that she is free and
does not like to subject herself to anyone else: "tengo libre
condición y no gusto de sujetarme" (1.14.187–88). For Marcela, freedom is incompatible with marriage, since marriage
demands that the wife obey her husband.

The view of marriage Marcela rejects was generally accepted at the time, not only in Spain but also in England and
in the rest of Europe. In his popular manual *La perfecta
casada* (The Perfect Wife), first published in 1583, Fray Luis
de León writes of the wife's duty to serve her husband, "ser-
vir al marido," and asserts that many women mistakenly

believe that exchanging a father's house for a husband's means exchanging slavery for liberty: "se engañan muchas mujeres, que piensan que el casarse no es más que dejar la casa del padre y pasarse a la del marido, y salir de servidumbre y venir a libertad y regalo" (1951, 233). In Cervantes' Spain, to reject marriage was tantamount to rejecting society itself. "The [nuclear] family," writes Michael Weisser,

> was, and continues to be, the core of life in the pueblo: many of the social conventions are designed to prepare one to form a family, to participate in a family, to continue existence through the family's economic or psychic legacy when it is dissolved. To reject the family—to remain unmarried or to take a partner without performing the social rites developed by the community—results in social ostracism, public scorn, and a legalized denial of rights and privileges in the community. (1976, 75)

Seventeenth-century Europe made no provision for a woman who refused either to marry or to become a nun. It was recognized that few women were suited to the rigors of the religious life; for the vast majority marriage was the only real option (Kelso 1956, 78, 91; Maclean 1980, 57, 66, 84). Because Marcela understands that society has no place for her, she chooses to become a shepherdess, rejecting the larger world of the village community for the little world of a community of shepherdesses that she can shape to her own desires.

In refusing to accept her place in the village community, Marcela rejects also the principle of hierarchical order that underlies so much of Renaissance thought. C. S. Lewis explains that

> Degrees of value are objectively present in the universe. Everything except God has some natural superior; everything except unformed matter has some natural infe-

rior. The goodness, happiness, and dignity of every being consists in obeying its natural superior and ruling its natural inferior. (1942, 72)

The idea of hierarchy underlies Renaissance thinking about marriage as it underlies Renaissance thinking about the proper functioning of the state. Husband and wife play quite different roles, as do the king and his subjects. In the *Coloquios matrimoniales* of the Erasmian Pedro de Luxán, first published in 1550 and reprinted ten times by 1589, we find the following bit of dialogue:

DOROCTEA. Como no eres casada?

EULALIA. Ni aun lo querria ser.

DOROCTEA. Por que causa no quieres tomar el yugo del matrimonio?

EULALIA. Algunas vezes he sido requerida por mis padres que me case y no lo he querido hazer.

DOROCTEA. Porque?

EULALIA. Porque no querria casarme.

DOROCTEA. Meterte monja?

EULALIA. Ni querria ser monja.

DOROCTEA. Porque?

EULALIA. Por no estar contino encerrada debaxo de siete llaves.

DOROCTEA. Pues que piensas de hazer no queriendo tomar estado ninguno: conviene a saber de ser casada o monja?

EULALIA. Bivir a ca [sic] en el mundo sin tener superior a quien dar cuenta: ni aun a quien contentar.

DOROCTEA. No te acabo de entender (1552, folio ii).

(DOROCTEA. How is it that you aren't married?

EULALIA. Nor do I want to be.

81

DOROCTEA. Why do you refuse the yoke of matri-
mony?

EULALIA. My parents have asked me more than
once to marry and I've always refused.

DOROCTEA. Why?

EULALIA. Because I didn't want to marry.

DOROCTEA. Did you want to become a nun?

EULALIA. No, I wouldn't like to be a nun either.

DOROCTEA. Why?

EULALIA. I wouldn't like to be shut up behind seven
locks.

DOROCTEA. Well, what *do* you intend to do if you
refuse either to marry or to become a nun?

EULALIA. To live in the world without any superior
to answer to or even try to please.

DOROCTEA. I can't understand you at all.)

Dorothea finds Eulalia's attitude incomprehensible, just as
Grisóstomo's friends refuse to take seriously Marcela's claim
that "tengo libre condición y no gusto de sujetarme."

For Marcela the freedom of the pastoral world is not freedom to love but freedom from love. She demands independ-
ence from any sort of human bond and thus denies the very
idea of Arcadia (Köhler 1966, 323). Marcela's insistence on
absolute autonomy keeps her from displaying—and worse
yet, from feeling—any sort of grief over the death of Grisóstomo. Her proud claim that she neither loves nor hates anyone—"ni quiero ni aborrezco a nadie" (1.14.188)—betrays a
terrible self-centeredness that renders her incapable of feeling
any real concern for anyone else.

All of this tends to undermine Marcela's assertion, at the
end of her defense, that "my desires are bounded by these
mountains, and if they go beyond them it is only to contem-
plate the beauty of the heavens, steps by which the soul

journeys toward its first home," "tienen mis deseos por tér-
mino estas montañas, y si de aquí salen, es a contemplar
la hermosura del cielo, pasos con que camina el alma a su
morada primera" (1.14.188). The religious overtones of her
peroration suggest a Platonic ascent from the solitary contem-
plation of the beauty of the natural world to a mystical con-
templation of the divine. And yet, as Renato Poggioli observes,

> we cannot take too seriously the claim Marcela makes
> at the end of her speech, when she says that one of her
> life tasks will be that heavenly contemplation which
> initiates a mortal's soul into its immortal bliss.... Be-
> fore that single, final allusion to the contemplation of
> Heaven, she has spoken far more extensively and elo-
> quently of the contemplation of nature, which she con-
> siders the most suitable mirror for reflecting the beauty
> of her own soul. In brief, not unlike the devotees of
> Eros, she treats her far less carnal but no less profane
> passion as if it were a form of sacred love. (1975, 174)

Marcela does not try to deceive the shepherds about her motives for rejecting Grisóstomo; she deceives herself about
their true nature. Like Don Quixote, she fails to distinguish
between what is possible in literature and what is possible in
real life.

Cervantes does not take sides with Marcela against Grisóstomo or with Grisóstomo against Marcela. Both are victims
of absurd conceptions learned from books. Grisóstomo remains faithful to the conception of love that dominated Spanish fifteenth-century courtly literature and that remained
very much alive in the following century, thanks to the suc-
cessive revisions and reprintings of the *Cancionero general*,
first published in 1511, and to the many inexpensive chap-

books that made individual poems or small groups of poems accessible to a wide audience.

The dangers of trying to live by such a notion of love are explored in a number of important sixteenth-century Italian and Spanish works. In Castiglione's *Book of the Courtier*, Ottaviano Fregoso declares that he has been frightened away from love by the laments of certain lovers whose eyes reveal their unhappiness:

> Se parlano, accompagnando ogni parola con certi sospiri triplicati, di null'altra cosa ragionano che di lacrime, di tormenti, di disperazioni e desidèri di morte; di modo che, se talor qualche scintilla amorosa pur mi s'è accesa nel core, io sùbito sònomi sforzato con ogni industria di spegnerla, non per odio ch'io porti alle donne . . . ma per mia salute. (1.10.96–97)

> (Whenever they speak, they accompany every word with tripled sighs and talk of nothing but tears, torments, despairs, and longings for death. So that even if at times any spark of love did kindle my heart, I have immediately made every effort to extinguish it, not out of any hate that I feel towards women . . . but for my own good.) (Singleton 1959, 23)

The dangers of surrender to love are clear in Ariosto's Orlando, whose madness Don Quixote finds so exemplary that he considers imitating it in his penance on the Peña Pobre, though he finally decides that Amadís offers an easier model (1.25). Ariosto, however, does not present Orlando as admirable, but insists instead that his madness reduces him to the level of a wild beast. Orlando's madness became the model for that of Albanio in Garcilaso's Second Eclogue, a work Cervantes knew and admired. R. O. Jones has seen the Second Eclogue as evidence that "for Garcilaso unhappy love had come to seem a sign of a moral disorder, and that he rejects the cult of despair which fills the *cancioneros*" (1966, 538). A similar attitude toward love is found in Gil Polo's pastoral novel *Diana enamorada*, another work Cervantes admired greatly; the priest spares it from the flames when Don Quixote's library is burned, ordering that it be treated as if it were by Apollo himself, "se guarde como si fuera del mesmo Apolo" (1.6.119). Like Ariosto and Garcilaso, Gil Polo refuses to believe that the lover's suffering ennobles him. He sees despair not as an indication of sensibility but of lack of sense. Góngora seems to have felt much the same way (Hart 1977, 219–20). By the time part 1 of *Don Quixote* appeared in 1605 many readers must have thought the love idealized in the *cancioneros* as absurdly old-fashioned as the chivalry idealized in the *libros de caballerías*.

Grisóstomo is not alone in remaining faithful to the older view of love as martyrdom. His view is shared by his friend Ambrosio and the other young men who follow Grisóstomo's example by becoming shepherds. All of them consider Grisóstomo an exemplary lover, as does Don Quixote, who spends the greater part of the night after his encounter with Marcela thinking of his lady Dulcinea in imitation of Marcela's suitors, "a imitación de los amantes de Marcela" (1.12.167).

Though Ambrosio and his friends concede that Marcela has given Grisóstomo no cause for jealousy, they refuse to accept her claim that she is not responsible for his death. Ambrosio now announces his intention to have Grisóstomo's grave marked by a stone for which he has composed the following epitaph:

> Yace aquí de un amador
> el mísero cuerpo helado,
> que fue pastor de ganado,

perdido por desamor.
Murió a manos del rigor
de una esquiva hermosa ingrata,
con quien su imperio dilata
la tiranía de amor. (1.14.188–89)

(Here lies the wretched cold body of a lover, who became a shepherd, destroyed by disdain. He died because of the rigidity of an ungrateful and arrogant beauty, through whom love extends the tyranny of his empire.)

Ambrosio's epitaph repeats the charges Grisóstomo himself had made against Marcela in his "versos desesperados." Nothing Marcela has said has persuaded Ambrosio to modify his view of her character or to absolve her of responsibility for his friend's death.

THAT the experiment in pastoral life initiated by Marcela leads nowhere is shown by its reappearance toward the end of part 1 in the story told by Eugenio, another wealthy young man turned goatherd. His name is of course symbolic; it means "well-born", as Grisóstomo (from the Greek saint's name *Chrysostomos*, literally "golden-mouthed") means "eloquent," ironically in view of Grisóstomo's failure to persuade Marcela to return his love. Eugenio has become a goatherd because of his love for Leandra, as Grisóstomo became a shepherd for love of Marcela. Like Marcela, Leandra is the daughter of a wealthy villager. Eugenio and another young man, Anselmo, have asked for her hand, and since both suitors are rich and of good family, her father has left the choice to her. Leandra, however, is in no hurry to make up her mind. While Eugenio and Anselmo await her decision, the son of a local peasant, Vicente de la Rosa, returns to the village, from which he had run away twelve years before as a boy of twelve. Vicente has been a soldier and is full of stories about his adventures. He also knows how to play the guitar and is something of a poet. Leandra finds him irresistible and runs off with him, taking with her a large sum of money and valuable jewels. Three days later she is discovered abandoned in a cave. Vicente has taken the money and the jewels, but Leandra insists so vehemently that he has not had intercourse with her that her father and suitors end by believing her. Leandra is packed off to a nearby convent to give the scandal a chance to quiet down, and Eugenio and Anselmo decide to become shepherds so that they can devote all their time to savoring their emotions. Eugenio's account of their decision and its aftermath recalls Pedro's description of the pastoral community founded by Grisóstomo. This time, the comic effect is even more pronounced, because of the almost mechanical repetition of the earlier passage and the difference in temperament and conduct between Leandra and Marcela. So many young men have followed the lead of Eugenio and Anselmo and become shepherds for love of Leandra that

parece que este sitio se ha convertido en la pastoral Arcadia, según está colmo de pastores y de apriscos, y no hay parte en él donde no se oiga el nombre de la hermosa Leandra. Éste la maldice y la llama antojadiza, varia y deshonesta; aquél la condena por fácil y ligera; tal la absuelve y perdona, y tal la justicia y vitupera; uno celebra su hermosura, otro reniega de su condición, y, en fin, todos la deshonran, y todos la adoran, y de todos se estiende a tanto la locura, que hay quien se queje de desdén sin haberla jamás hablado, y aun quien se lamente y sienta la rabiosa enfermedad de los celos, que ella jamás dio a nadie.... No hay hueco de peña, ni margen de arroyo, ni sombra de árbol que no esté ocupada de algún pastor que sus desventuras a los aires cuente; el eco repite el nombre de Leandra dondequiera

87

que pueda formarse: Leandra resuenan los montes, Leandra murmuran los arroyos, y Leandra nos tiene a todos suspensos y encantados, esperando sin esperanza y temiendo sin saber de qué tememos. (1.51.595)

(It seems that this place has been turned into the pastoral Arcady, full of shepherds and folds, and there isn't a spot in it where one doesn't hear the name of the fair Leandra. One curses her and calls her capricious, fickle and lascivious; another accuses her of being wanton and frivolous; this one pardons and absolves her and that one condemns and abuses her; one praises her beauty and another reproaches her for her conduct. In short, all abuse her and all adore her, and their madness has gone so far that some who have never spoken to her complain that she has rejected them, and some lament and feel the raging fever of jealousy, though she never gave anyone cause to be jealous.... There is no hollow among the rocks, no bank of a stream, no shady spot under a tree that is not occupied by some shepherd telling his misfortunes to the winds; every echo repeats the name of Leandra, the mountains resound with "Leandra," the streams murmur "Leandra," and Leandra keeps us all on tenterhooks and bewitched, hoping without hope and afraid without knowing what we fear.)

Significantly, the end of Eugenio's story is left up in the air, like the story of Marcela and her army of suitors. Eugenio's hatred for all women is as sterile as the unrequited love of Grisóstomo and his friends for one particular woman.

Toward the end of part 2, Don Quixote and Sancho discover still another "pastoral Arcady." As they make their way toward Barcelona after taking leave of the Duke and Duchess, they pass through a wood where Don Quixote becomes entangled in some nets stretched between the trees. While he

is struggling to free himself, he is approached by two shepherdesses, or rather two young women dressed as shepherdesses, for the elegance of their clothing shows that they are
not country folk. They explain to Don Quixote that the nets
are not meant for him, but have been set up to catch birds,
and then go on to tell him who they are and what they are
doing there:

> En una aldea que está hasta dos leguas de aquí, donde
> hay mucha gente principal y muchos hidalgos y ricos,
> entre muchos amigos y parientes se concertó que con sus
> hijos, mujeres y hijas, vecinos, amigos y parientes, nos
> viniésemos a holgar a este sitio, que es uno de los más
> agradables de todos estos contornos, formando entre
> todos una nueva y pastoril Arcadia, vistiéndonos las
> doncellas de zagalas y los mancebos de pastores.
> Traemos estudiadas dos églogas, una del famoso poeta
> Garcilaso, y otra del excelentísimo Camoes, en su misma
> lengua portuguesa, las cuales hasta ahora no hemos
> representado. Ayer fue el primer día que aquí llegamos;
> tenemos entre estos ramos plantadas algunas tiendas,
> que dicen se llaman de campaña, en el margen de un
> abundoso arroyo que todos estos prados fertiliza; tendi-
> mos la noche pasada estas redes de estos árboles para
> engañar los simples pajarillos que, ojeados con nuestro
> ruido, vinieren a dar en ellas. Si gustáis, señor, de ser
> nuestro huésped, seréis agasajado liberal y cortésmente;
> porque por agora en este sitio no ha de entrar la pesa-
> dumbre ni la melancolía. (2.58.477)

(In a village about two leagues off, where there are
many people of wealth and breeding, many friends and
relatives agreed to come, accompanied by their wives,
children, friends, and relatives, for a holiday in this spot,
which is one of the pleasantest around here, and to

establish a new pastoral Arcady, we girls dressing up as shepherdesses and the boys as shepherds. We have prepared two eclogues, one by the famous poet Garcilaso and the other by the excellent Camoens, in the original Portuguese, but we have not yet performed them. Yesterday was our first day here; we have a few of what they call field-tents set up among these trees along the bank of an abundant stream that waters all these meadows; last night we stretched these nets between these trees to catch the innocent little birds that will fly into them frightened by the noise we make. If you, sir, would like to be our guest, you will be received most hospitably and courteously, for now neither grief nor melancholy shall enter this place.)

The first pastoral community that Don Quixote encounters in part 1, the one that came into being as a result of Marcela's decision to become a shepherdess, is really two separate communities, one composed of men and the other of women: Grisóstomo's followers are "ricos mancebos, hidalgos y labradores," Marcela's "las demás zagalas del lugar." Though the two communities do not live in isolation from one another, they do not form parts of a single larger community. The "new pastoral Arcady" that Don Quixote finds on the road to Barcelona is quite different. It is not made up only of young men or young women; on the contrary, it consists of whole families. Still more important, it does not represent a flight from life in the village but only a temporary interruption of it, a sort of holiday camp, undertaken for the sake of recreation. For these villagers, the pastoral life is a form of make-believe, like their performances of eclogues by Garcilaso and Camoens.

What sets the "new pastoral Arcady" apart from the pastoral communities centered on Grisóstomo and Eugenio is the absence of despair. When the shepherdesses invite Don Quixote to join them they assure him that "now neither grief nor melancholy shall enter this place." The new Arcadians know how to distinguish between art and life, something the inhabitants of the first two pastoral Arcadies fail to do and, of course, something Don Quixote also fails to do when he tries to imitate the heroes of the romances of chivalry.

Don Quixote refuses the New Arcadians' invitation to join them and continues on his way to Barcelona, where he encounters the Knight of the White Moon, later revealed to the reader, though not to Don Quixote himself, as Sansón Carrasco. The Knight challenges Don Quixote to single combat and makes him swear that he will abandon knight-errantry for a year if he is defeated, as of course he is (2.64.532–33). As Don Quixote and Sancho are returning home, they again pass through the wood which had been the site of the "new pastoral Arcady." Seeing it prompts Don Quixote to propose to Sancho that they become shepherds themselves:

Éste es el prado donde topamos a las bizarras pastoras y gallardos pastores que en él querían renovar e imitar a la pastoral Arcadia, pensamiento tan nuevo como discreto, a cuya imitación, si es que a ti te parece bien, querría, ¡ oh Sancho!, que nos convirtiésemos en pastores, siquiera el tiempo que tengo de estar recogido. Yo compraré algunas ovejas, y todas las demás cosas que al pastoral ejercicio son necesarias, y llamándome yo *el pastor Quijotiz* y tú *el pastor Pancino*, nos andaremos por los montes, por las selvas y por los prados, cantando aquí, endechando allí, bebiendo de los líquidos cristales de las fuentes, o ya de los limpios arroyuelos, o de los caudalosos ríos. Daránnos con abundantísima mano de su dulcísimo fruto las encinas, asiento los troncos de los durísimos alcornoques, sombra los sauces, olor las rosas,

alfombras de mil colores matizadas los estendidos prados, aliento el aire claro y puro, luz la luna y las estrellas,
a pesar de la escuridad de la noche; gusto el canto,
alegría el lloro, Apolo versos, el amor conceptos, con que
podremos hacernos eternos y famosos, no sólo en los
presentes, sino en los venideros siglos. (2.67.548)

(This is the place where we met those splendid shepherdesses and gallant shepherds who were trying to revive and imitate pastoral Arcady, an idea as original as
it was intelligent, in imitation of which, if you, Sancho,
approve, I should like us to become shepherds, at least
for as long as I must remain in retirement. I shall buy
some sheep and everything else needed for the pastoral
calling and the two of us, I as the shepherd Quixotiz and
you as the shepherd Pancino, will roam the forests,
woods, and meadows, singing songs here, lamenting
there, drinking from the crystal waters of the springs or
the limpid brooks or the flowing rivers. The oaks will
offer us their sweet fruit with a lavish hand; the trunks
of the hard cork trees, a seat; the willows, shade; the
roses, fragrance; the broad meadows, carpets woven of
a thousand colors; the clear pure air, breath; the moon
and stars, light amidst the darkness of the night; singing, pleasure; weeping, joy; Apollo, verses; and love,
conceits, with which we shall make ourselves famous,
not only in the present age but also in ages still to come.)

Don Quixote's enthusiastic description of pastoral life is
marked by new language, just as his first appearances as a
knight-errant are marked by a liberal use of the archaic
speech forms found in the romances of chivalry (Mancing
1982, 15–32). Don Quixote's praise of pastoral life is full of
syntactic parallelism and of adjectives, the latter usually
placed before the noun they modify (*líquidos cristales, limpios*

92

arroyuelos, caudalosos ríos) and often in their absolute superlative form (*abundantísima mano, dulcísimo fruto, durísimos alcornoques*). There is every reason to believe him when he tells Sancho that he is something of a poet, "algún tanto poeta." Like the new Arcadians, Don Quixote in this instance can distinguish between art and life, as indeed he usually can in everything that does not involve knight-errantry. He does not propose to become a shepherd but only to play at being one for a fixed period of time, "as long as I must remain in retirement." Though the songs he and his friends will compose in their pastoral disguises may be sad ones, like those sung by the shepherds in Garcilaso's eclogues, Don Quixote emphasizes to Sancho the pleasure of composing them. The pleasure is all the greater in that these mock shepherds, with the possible exception of Don Quixote himself, will choose their themes without reference to any emotions that they have actually experienced:

> Yo me quejaré de ausencia; tú te alabarás de firme enamorado; el pastor Carrascón, de desdeñado; y el cura Curiambro, de lo que él más puede servirse, y así, andará la cosa que no haya más que desear. (2.67.550)

> (I shall lament my lady's absence; you, Sancho, will boast of your constancy; the shepherd Carrascón will be a rejected lover; and the curate Curiambro will sing about anything he likes, and so everything will be arranged to our hearts' content.)

The pastoral life celebrated in the poetic tradition is attractive in much the same way as chivalric life. It becomes dangerous only if it is accepted uncritically as a guide to conduct. Viewed simply as an afternoon's diversion, as it is by the new Arcadians and by Don Quixote in his projected life as the shepherd Quixotiz it is harmless and may even be salutary.

In the prologue to the *Novelas ejemplares* Cervantes explains that

> Mi intento ha sido poner en la plaza de nuestra república una mesa de trucos, donde cada uno puede llegar a entretenerse, sin daño de barras; digo sin daño del alma ni del cuerpo, porque los ejercicios honestos y agradables, antes aprovechan que dañan.
>
> Sí, que no siempre se está en los templos, no siempre se ocupan los oratorios; no siempre se asiste a los negocios, por calificados que sean. Horas hay de recreación, donde el afligido espíritu descanse. (1.64)

> (My intention has been to set up a billiard table in the public square of our nation where everyone can come to entertain himself without damage to anyone.
>
> For certainly people aren't always in church; the oratories aren't always full; people aren't always engaged in business, however important it may be. There are times for recreation, when the weary spirit may rest.)

A recent study by Bruce Wardropper (1982) connects this passage with the *aprobación* included in the first edition of the *Novelas ejemplares*, published in Madrid by Juan de la Cuesta in 1613. The aprobación is signed by one of Cervantes' friends, the Trinitarian friar Juan Bautista Capataz, whom Cervantes praises as a poet in his *Viaje del Parnaso*, and it is quite possible that it presents a point of view suggested by Cervantes himself. Fray Juan declares that Cervantes' *Novelas* embody the Christian virtue of eutrapelia:

> He visto y leído las doce *Novelas ejemplares* compuestas por Miguel de Cervantes Saavedra; y supuesto que es sentencia llana del angélico doctor Santo Tomás, que la eutropelia [sic] es virtud, la que consiste en un entretenimiento honesto, juzgo que la verdadera eutropelia

está en estas *Novelas*, porque entretienen con su nove-
dad, enseñan con sus ejemplos a huir vicios y seguir
virtudes, y el autor cumple con su intento, con que da
honra a nuestra lengua castellana, y avisa a las repúblicas
de los daños que de algunos vicios se siguen, con otras
muchas comodidades, y así me parece se le puede y debe
dar la licencia que pide. (1.55)

(I have seen and read the twelve *Exemplary Stories* composed by Miguel de Cervantes Saavedra, and since it is
plainly said by the angelic doctor Saint Thomas [Aqui-
nas] that eutrapelia is a virtue that consists of wholesome
recreation, I judge that true eutrapelia is to be found in
these *Stories*, for they entertain with their novelty [and]
teach with their examples how to shun vices and practice virtues, and the author has achieved his intention,
giving honor to our Castilian tongue and warning the
nation of the damage that may be caused by certain
vices, together with many other merits, so that I believe
he can and should be given the permission to print that
he requests.)

Long forgotten except by historians of theology, eutrapelia is
both a temporary respite from more serious concerns and a
preparation for returning to them with renewed strength.
Wardropper notes the probability that Cervantes' own title
for his collection was *Novelas ejemplares, de honestísima re-
creación* (1982, 165). We are close to the *Vergnüge und Erholung* that Erich Auerbach found in *Don Quixote*. The "new
pastoral Arcady" Don Quixote visits on his way to Barcelona
represents eutrapelia in action, as does his plan to set up his
own pastoral Arcady as the shepherd Quixotiz.

CHAPTER VI

"Disprayse of a Courtly Life"

Cervantes' treatment of pastoral love in part 1 of *Don Quixote* is only one of a number of pastoral elements in the novel. In part 2 he offers an elaborate treatment of another traditional pastoral theme, the contrast between country life and life at court. As in his treatment of pastoral love in part 1, he returns to a theme he had dealt with before, in the song composed by Lauso, a courtier turned shepherd, and sung by Damón near the beginning of book 4 of *La Galatea*.

The contrast between court and country found in so many Renaissance pastorals rests on an ideal of the good life, the state of contentment that in classical Latin was called *otium*. The connotations of the Latin word are quite different from those of its English derivative *otiose* or those of modern Spanish *ocioso*. They include idleness, but idleness conceived not as absence of activity, but rather as freedom to pursue one's thoughts and develop one's character unconstrained by practical considerations. The primary meaning of otium is thus "leisure, time to do whatever one likes." An important secondary meaning has to do with the qualities of peace, repose, and quietness that result not just from having time on one's hands, but from using that time wisely by learning to exercise one's own best qualities. "Elizabethan pastoral poetry," writes Hallett Smith, "is essentially a celebration ... of *otium*." The opposite of the ideal of otium and of being content with little is the kind of ambition that in sixteenth-century England was often called "the aspiring mind." "The central meaning of pastoral," Smith asserts, "is the rejection of the aspiring mind" (1952, 8–10).

At the beginning of the seventeenth century the word "ambition," like its Spanish counterpart *ambición*, normally meant "excessive ambition," condemned as a manifestation of the aspiring mind. Shakespeare offers many examples. *The Oxford English Dictionary* cites Cardinal Woolsey's words in *King Henry the Eighth*: "Cromwell, I charge thee, fling away ambition! By that sin fell the angels" (2.3). The *Diccionario de autoridades* cites texts from Góngora and Diego de Saavedra to exemplify the word's primary meaning, which it defines as "passión *desreglada* de conseguir honras, dignidades, hacienda y conveniencias" (italics mine). In his great Spanish dictionary published in 1611, Covarrubias similarly defines ambición as "una codicia demasiada y diligencia extraordinaria en alcançar grandes honras y mandos, dignidades y magistrados; porque los tales ambiciosos van y vienen, buelven, rodean y trastornan el mundo a fin de salir con sus pretensiones."

Such an attitude toward individual ambition implies, of course, that in an ideal society the individual's place remains fixed once and for all. Anyone who dares to claim a social status that is not his by birth risks inviting censure. Don Quixote, of course, or rather Alonso Quijano, is one of those who dare to do so. He is an hidalgo who insists that he is a caballero, an insistence his niece finds as absurd as his attempt to revive the practice of knight-errantry:

> —¡Válame Dios!—dijo la sobrina—. ¡Que sepa vuestra merced tanto, señor tío, ... y que, con todo esto, dé en una ceguera tan grande y en una sandez tan conocida, que se dé a entender que es ... caballero, no lo siendo, porque aunque lo puedan ser los hidalgos, no lo son los pobres! (2.6.82)

> ("Good Lord!" said his niece. "How can you know so much, uncle, ... and still be capable of such great blind-

ness and such obvious foolishness as pretending to be
... a knight when you're not one, for even if hidalgos
can be knights, poor ones can't!")

When Don Quixote asks Sancho to tell him what people in
the village are saying about his plan to revive knight-errantry, Sancho replies that

> Los hidalgos dicen que no conteniéndose vuestra merced
> en los límites de la hidalguía, se ha puesto *don* y se ha
> arremetido a caballero con cuatro cepas y dos yugadas
> de tierra y con un trapo atrás y otro adelante (2.2.56).

(The hidalgos say you haven't been satisfied with staying
within the limits of your class but have taken to calling
yourself "Don" and claiming to be a knight when you
have only four vines and two plots of land and nothing
to wear but a rag in front and another in back.)

The hierarchical order of society was never questioned even
by the most clear-sighted of the arbitristas. "One of the great
themes of González de Cellorigo's treatise," writes J. H. Elliott, "was that things had gone wrong because the social
balance had been upset—all moderation and just proportion
had gone, as men aspired to a higher social status than that
of their fathers. This was a commonplace of the times, repeated by *arbitristas* and royal ministers and echoed by playwrights" (1977, 56).

Though the rejection of the aspiring mind is one of the
central themes of part 2 of *Don Quixote*, Cervantes, as he
usually does in his greatest book, treats his traditional materials in a way all his own. He assigns the rejection of the
aspiring mind to Sancho, a peasant very different from any
of the current literary stereotypes.

Cervantes' portrait of Sancho combines two contrasting
types found in the sixteenth-century Spanish theater and in

the continuations of *La Celestina* (Hendrix 1925). One type is stupid, credulous, cowardly, and has an inordinate interest in food, drink, and sleep. He speaks in dialect, treats his superiors with excessive familiarity, and dreams of grotesquely inflated rewards for his services. The other type is given to sarcastic asides, is the friend and confidant of his master, and often takes matters into his own hands. Cervantes does more than combine traits from the two traditional types; he presents Sancho as an eloquent though untutored spokesman for Christian values, rather than a crude materialist ridiculed for his ignorance of even the most basic Christian doctrines. Cervantes also turns aside from earlier treatments by presenting Sancho not as a cuckold but as an exemplary husband and father (Márquez Villanueva 1973, 84–85). In stressing Sancho's concern for his family, Cervantes breaks away from literary tradition and attaches himself to a more broadly based moral tradition. In sixteenth-century Spain, as Michael R. Weisser notes, "the peasant family was an object of cultural veneration by the society at large.... Taking his cue from earlier pastoral writings, [Fray] Luis de León elevated the peasant family to an ideal of near sainthood.... The peasant household became the moral yardstick for measuring all other life-styles in society" (1976, 75).

Though Sancho at first resists Don Quixote's attempts to improve his speech and table manners, he gradually comes to accept much of Don Quixote's teaching. In his delightful conversation with his wife Teresa in part 2, chapter 5, Sancho reproaches her for adopting precisely the same attitude he himself had shown earlier, in a splendid example of the analogous actions discussed in our second chapter. Teresa's stubbornness and Sancho's growing irritation at the difficulty of persuading her to share his ambitions combine to make one of the finest comic scenes in the novel as well as a superb illustration of Cervantes' ability to do something Ariosto does not attempt to do: trace the impact of experience on an individual temperament.

SANCHO'S initial reluctance to accept Don Quixote as a teacher of manners, like Teresa's reluctance to accept her husband in the same role, is not based on moral grounds, as in more conventional attacks on courtly life, but on his fear of making himself ridiculous, an attitude still found among Spanish peasants today, according to the social anthropologist Carmelo Lisón Toledano (1966, 339–41). Sancho's reluctance to change his ways is doubtless related also to what another anthropologist, George Foster, has called the "Image of Limited Good". Foster explains that

> by "Image of Limited Good" I mean that broad areas of peasant behavior are patterned in such fashion as to suggest that peasants view their ... total environment ... as one in in which all the desired things of life such as land, wealth, health, friendship and love, manliness and honor, respect and status, power and influence, security and safety, *exist in finite quantity* and *are always in short supply*.... Not only do these and all other "good things" exist in finite and limited quantities, but in addition *there is no way directly within peasant power to increase the available quantities*. It is as if the obvious fact of land shortage in a densely populated area applied to all other desired things: not enough to go around (1965, 296)

It is understandable that an individual peasant who sees no possibility of bettering his situation will resist any suggestion that he should change his behavior. His adaptability, however, may increase if he has reason to believe that his situation can change, and this of course is just what happens in the case of Sancho.

Sancho's perception of his situation changes when he begins to take more seriously Don Quixote's promise to make him governor of an *ínsula*. He has no clear idea of what an ínsula is—the usual Spanish term for island is *isla*—and he has doubts about Don Quixote's ability to keep his promise, but his doubts are dispelled when the Duke and Duchess make him governor of Barataria. In presenting Sancho as a peasant who, after some initial resistance, doggedly and sometimes successfully tries to imitate the speech and manners of his betters, Cervantes displays an acute perception of contemporary social reality. Michael Weisser has observed that inventories of household possessions in a seventeenth-century Castilian peasant community reveal that

> Even the poorest peasants were aware of the culture and life-styles of the outside world as they filtered down from the village elite through the middle class and into their own homes. The image of the rural dweller as being cognizant of urban values, yet rejecting them ... was absent from the actual rural scene. ... Contrary to rejecting urban mores and styles, the peasantry adopted and adapted them to fit the realities of rural life (1976, 53).

Weisser's observations confirm the view first formulated by the anthropologist A. L. Kroeber that "peasants constitute part-societies with part-cultures. [They are] definitely rural—yet live in relation to market towns; they form a class segment of a larger population which usually contains also urban centers" (1948, 284). Kroeber's insight has been developed by other anthropologists. Robert Redfield, for example, asserts that "the culture of a peasant community ... is not autonomous ... ; to maintain itself peasant culture requires continual communication to the local community of thought originating outside of it. The intellectual and often the religious and moral life of the peasant village is perpetually incomplete" (1956, 68). Peasant society is marked by the relationship between what Redfield calls the "great tradition of the reflective few" and the "little tradition of the largely unreflective many" (ibid., 70).

It may have been a perception of the connection between the great tradition of urban or courtly society and the little tradition of the countryside that led many Renaissance writers to suggest that a stay in a pastoral community might serve not only as a respite from the stress of life at court but also as a preparation for return to it. If courtly values were completely different from the values that shape the life of the pastoral community, courtiers could learn nothing from shepherds. Though most Renaissance writers' interest in how real peasants lived was extremely limited, there was a widespread conviction that the peasants' life-style embodied values to which urban society paid only lip service, the traditional theme of *menosprecio de la corte y alabanza de aldea* treated in Sir Philip Sidney's poem "Disprayse of a Courtly Life" (1962, 262–64).

Cervantes takes up the theme of menosprecio de la corte in his account of the visit of Don Quixote and Sancho to the palace of the Duke and Duchess. Some critics have treated the Duke and Duchess very badly. Vladimir Nabokov calls them "the main pair of villainous enchanters in the book" and says that "the cruelty of the book reaches here atrocious heights" (1983, 62). The Duke and Duchess come in for a fair amount of criticism in *Don Quixote* itself. The Duke's chaplain reproaches him for amusing himself with his mad guest:

> Vuestra excelencia, señor mío, tiene que dar cuenta a nuestro Señor de lo que hace este buen hombre. Este don Quijote, o don Tonto, o como se llama, imagino yo que no debe de ser tan mentecato como vuestra excelen-

cia quiere que sea, dándole ocasiones a la mano para que
lleve adelante sus sandeces y vaciedades. (2.31.281–82)

(My lord, you must give account to Our Lord for what
this good man does. I imagine that this Don Quixote, or
Don Dolt, or whatever he calls himself, is not so great
a fool as you would have him be by encouraging him to
go ahead with his foolishness and nonsense.)

But this "grave ecclesiastic" is an irritable bigot who addresses Don Quixote a moment later as "you poor simpleton"
(*alma de cántaro*). Cervantes introduces him by calling him

destos que gobiernan las casas de los príncipes; destos
que, como no nacen príncipes, no aciertan a enseñar
cómo lo han de ser los que lo son; destos que quieren
que la grandeza de los grandes se mida con la estrecheza
de sus ánimos. (2.31.278)

(one of those who rule princes' households; one of those
who, not being princes themselves, never succeed in
teaching proper behavior to those who are; one of those
who would have the greatness of a nobleman measured
by their own narrow-mindedness.)

We can hardly take this priest's censure of his master at face
value, and the same is true of Cide Hamete Benengeli's remark that he considers the Duke and Duchess as mad as their
guests since they went to so much trouble to play a trick on
two fools, "que tiene para sí ser tan locos los burladores como
los burlados, y que no estaban los duques dos dedos de pare-
cer tontos, pues tanto ahinco ponían en burlarse de dos tontos" (2.70.564–65). Don Quixote, though mad, is not a fool,
and Sancho, though certainly foolish in some ways, is just as
certainly not mad. Nor should we forget that Cide Hamete
is a Moor, and like other members of his race a liar.

Cervantes tells us nothing about what life in the ducal palace is like in ordinary circumstances. We see the Duke and Duchess only during a temporary holiday, a welcome break in the monotonous routine of a remote country house or castle, "casa de placer o castillo" (2.31.273), as Cervantes ambiguously calls it. Sancho's term as governor of Barataria takes place in an atmosphere Cervantes' contemporaries would have associated with the carnival season, in which the ordinary rules of social life were suspended (Redondo 1978; Riley 1986, 118–19). Though the Duke and Duchess are not praised as exemplary, they are not condemned as sadistic monsters. There is no reason to doubt the genuineness of their concern (2.46.386) when they learn that the cats in the "temeroso espanto cencerril y gatuno" have scratched Don Quixote's face so badly that he must stay in bed for a week. The amusement they seek from their strange guests is comparable to that sought by Don Quixote's host in Barcelona, Don Antonio Moreno, who reproaches Sansón Carrasco for attempting to restore the mad knight to sanity:

> —¡Oh, señor ... Dios os perdone el agravio que habéis hecho a todo el mundo en querer volver cuerdo al más gracioso loco que hay en él! ¿No veis, señor, que no podrá llegar el provecho que cause la cordura de don Quijote a lo que llega el gusto que da con sus desvaríos? ... y si no fuese contra caridad, diría que nunca sane don Quijote, porque con su salud, no solamente perdemos sus gracias, sino las de Sancho Panza su escudero, que cualquiera dellas puede volver a alegrar a la misma melancolía—. (2.65.536–37)

> ("Oh, sir, ... may God forgive you for the offense you have committed against the whole world by trying to make sane the most amusing madman to be found in it!

Don't you see, sir, that any benefit that may come from Don Quixote's sanity can never equal the pleasure he gives with his follies? And if it were not uncharitable I would say that Don Quixote should never be cured, for his recovery would make us lose not only his own amusing remarks but those of his squire Sancho Panza, any one of which could cheer up melancholy itself.)

No one would disagree with William Empson when he remarks that "no doubt it was crude to keep a lunatic as a pet," but Empson goes on to observe that "we may call Shakespeare and Velasquez in evidence that the interest was not as trivial as it was brutal" (1935, 47). Perhaps the Duke and Duchess amuse themselves with Don Quixote for much the same reasons that prompted Velázquez to undertake the remarkable series of portraits of dwarfs and mental defectives now in the Prado. Velázquez, an ambitious and successful courtier as well as a great painter, would not have dared to mock the tastes of his patrons despite his evident sympathy for the subjects of his portraits.

Don Quixote's madness, which so many modern readers find embarrassing and so many critics ignore, helps to confer on his words and actions the quality of *admiratio* that makes them so amusing to his companions. There is no modern equivalent for admiratio. E. C. Riley defines it as "a sort of excitement stimulated by whatever was exceptional, whether because of its novelty, its excellence, or other extreme characteristics" (1962, 89). Many of Don Quixote's speeches and actions provoke admiratio because of their absurdity. On the other hand, some of his wiser pronouncements in his lucid intervals cause his listeners to feel surprise and wonder precisely because they do not expect to find wisdom in the words of a madman. Similarly, Sancho's decisions as governor of Barataria produce admiratio in those who hear them, since

courtiers do not expect to hear wise judgments from an ignorant peasant: "la sentencia ... movió a admiración a los
circunstantes" (2.45.378); "quedaron todos admirados"
(2.45.379); "los circunstantes quedaron admirados de nuevo
de los juicios y sentencias de su nuevo gobernador" (2.45.382).

Though life at the ducal castle is very different from that
at Urbino described by Castiglione in *The Book of the Courtier*, even at Urbino not all of the time was devoted to the
serious conversations Castiglione claims to have transcribed
in his nostalgic book: "poets, musicians, *and all sorts of buf-
foons*, and the most excellent of every kind of talent that
could be found in Italy, were always gathered there" (Singleton 1959, 17; italics mine).

A large part of Castiglione's book 2 is concerned with
showing how a courtier may display his wit to advantage,
both verbally and by playing tricks on others. Similarly, many
incidents in *Don Quixote* deal with tricks and hoaxes, as P. E.
Russell has noted (1969, 312). The tricks are usually at the
expense of Don Quixote or Sancho, though occasionally at
the expense of others like the barber who is persuaded by
Don Quixote's companions that his basin is really Mam-
brino's helmet (1.45). Many modern readers are dissatisfied
with part 2, in particular with the scenes at the ducal palace,
because they feel that Don Quixote and Sancho are the innocent victims of a series of pointless practical jokes. Cervantes'
contemporaries may have felt differently. Their attitude is
easier to understand, if not to justify, in the light of the
discussion of practical jokes in book 2 of Castiglione's *Courtier*. The future Cardinal Bernardo Bibbiena explains that

> Il termine e misura del far ridere mordendo bisogna
> ancor esser diligentemente considerato, e chi sia quello
> che si morde; perché non s'induce riso col dileggiar un
> misero e calamitoso, né ancora un ribaldo e scelerato

publico, perché questi par che meritino maggior castigo che l'esser burlati; e gli animi umani non sono inclinati a beffare i miseri, eccetto se quei tali nella sua infelicità non si vantassero e fossero superbi e prosuntuosi. . . . Però conveniente cosa è beffare e ridersi dei vizi collocati in persone né misere tanto che movano compassione, né tanto scelerate che paia che meritino esser condennate a pena capitale, né tanto grandi che un loro piccol sdegno possa far gran danno. (2.46.262)

(We must carefully consider the scope and the limits of provoking laughter by derision, and who it is that we deride; for laughter is not produced by poking fun at some poor unfortunate soul, nor at some rascal or open criminal, because these latter seem to deserve a punishment greater than ridicule; and we are not inclined to make sport of poor wretches unless they boast of their misfortune and are proud and presumptuous. . . . Yet it is proper to ridicule and laugh at the vices of those who are neither so wretched as to excite compassion, nor so wicked as to seem to deserve capital punishment, nor of so great a station that their wrath could do us much harm [Singleton 1959, 146].)

P. E. Russell notes that a "not inconsiderable number of seventeenth-century readers . . . far from feeling any sympathy for Don Quixote and Sancho, felt a positive dislike for them" (1969, 315). Don Quixote, after all, claims a social status that is not his by right, and the mere fact that Sancho is a peasant is enough to make him fair game, as is clear from Bibbiena's cruel anecdote about the one-eyed peasant who is cheated by a physician (2.77.302; Singleton 1959, 174). The visit of Don Quixote and Sancho to the country house of the Duke and Duchess is a variation on a plot found in

many Renaissance works, in which one of the principal characters spends some time in a rural setting quite different from
his or her usual environment. Cervantes himself had used it
in some of his *Novelas ejemplares* (Hart 1981). Rosalie Colie,
writing of pastoral drama, observes that

> This plot-form ... was so thoroughly identified with
> the pastoral that as a formula it could imply without
> overtly stating a great deal of standard pastoral thema-
> tics. Sheep, for instance, were often quite absent from
> such plays, which sometimes lacked even the pasture
> environment. But the *themes* associated with pastoral
> (court-country, art-nature, nature-nurture) could be
> counted on to inform plays with this plot-pattern. A plot
> on this plan, thus, was a recognizable vehicle for dis-
> course on the pastoral themes, an abstraction designed
> to interpret problems of nature and nurture originally
> associated with more overtly pastoral topics. (1974, 245)

The setting for a plot of this kind is what Renato Poggioli
calls a "pastoral oasis." The pastoral oasis is seldom the setting of an entire work. More often it is the setting for an
interlude, "a bucolic episode, which breaks the main action
or pattern, suspending for a while the heroic, romantic, or
pathetic mood of the whole" (1975, 9). One of the attractions
of such a pastoral interlude for Cervantes, and for many other
Renaissance writers, was that it provided an opportunity to
let characters assume unfamiliar roles. Its function is akin to
that of masquerade as set forth by Castiglione (2.11), for it
allows one to show flexibility by pretending to be someone
other than one's usual self, as Sancho does when he demonstrates that he knows how to rule wisely and justly in
Barataria.

Typically, the visitor to the pastoral community is a member of courtly society who adopts for a time the lifestyle of a

shepherd or shepherdess. In *As You Like It* Shakespeare contrasts the urbanity of Rosalind and the other fugitives from
the court with the crudeness of permanent residents of the
forest of Arden like Audrey and William, as Spenser in *The
Faerie Queene* contrasts Sir Calidore's polished manners with
the churlishness of Coridon. In *Don Quixote*, however, the
typical situation is turned upside down; the scene is not the
countryside but the court, and the visitors are not courtiers
but countrymen. Though Don Quixote is an hidalgo, it
is clear that neither he nor Sancho has had any previous experience of the kind of life offered them by the Duke and
Duchess.

In many Renaissance pastorals, the visitor from the court
meets someone who has had firsthand experience of life there
and has found it so little to his liking that he has returned to
the country. Most pastoral writers do not allow us to see the
experiences that lead one of their characters to feel dissatisfied
with life at court. They present the experiences as part of the
antecedent action, often as an account of his past life given by
the character himself. Thus, in book 6, canto 9 of *The Faerie
Queene*, Spenser makes Meliboee tell Sir Calidore the reasons
that prompted him to return from the court to the country,
and Spenser's model Tasso, in canto 7 of his *Gerusalemme
liberata*, has the old shepherd who welcomes Erminia to the
pastoral world tell her about the shortcomings of life at court.
Cervantes, however, lets us see for ourselves the experiences
that lead Sancho to reject his own earlier ambitions. This,
coupled with the fact that we know a great deal about Sancho
from having watched him develop through a whole series of
adventures as Don Quixote's squire, gives Cervantes' treatment a flavor all its own.

As in other Renaissance pastorals, both Don Quixote and
Sancho move, in C. L. Barber's well-known phrase, "through
release to clarification" (1959, 6). Part 2 differs from part 1 in

that both Don Quixote and Sancho experience a kind of *desengaño*. The frequent translation of the Spanish word as "disillusion" is apt to be misleading. The achievement of desengaño is desirable, an awakening to reality. It means seeing things as they are and seeing oneself as one really is. The visit to the Duke and Duchess marks a step toward desengaño for both Don Quixote and Sancho. One reason part 2 failed to match the immense success of part 1—part 1 was printed fourteen times before 1650, part 2 only seven— may be that the second part failed to match the expectations of readers of the first, who were surprised and no doubt disappointed to find in it a more serious treatment of Don Quixote and Sancho than the first part had led them to expect (Chevalier 1981, 119).

Thanks to the Duke and Duchess, Sancho does become governor of an ínsula, just as Don Quixote had promised, and shows that he has all the qualities needed to govern it well. His lack of education—he does not know how to read or write—turns out to be no handicap. Becoming governor of Barataria does not, however, bring Sancho the happiness that he had imagined. The court physician Dr. Pedro Recio de Agüero (his name recalls the phrase *de mal agüero* "ill-omened"), who comes from Tirteafuera (Take-'em-away), refuses to let him eat or drink what he wants, insisting, for example, that there is nothing less nourishing than stew, "no hay cosa en el mundo de peor mantenimiento que una olla podrida" (2.47.388). Sancho's experience as governor teaches him the value of the freedom he had enjoyed as a simple peasant. When he renounces his governorship, he takes his leave of Barataria asking only to be allowed to return to his former liberty and to be reborn from the death that the governorship has been for him: "Abrid camino, señores míos, y dejadme volver a mi antigua libertad, dejadme que vaya a buscar la vida pasada, para que me resucite de esta muerte

110

presente" (2.53.444). The imagery of death and resurrection in Sancho's farewell speech is underscored by his fall into a pit and his subsequent rescue by Don Quixote in chapter 55.

FOR Don Quixote, too, his visit to the Duke and Duchess seems at first to realize the dream that has sustained him through all the hardships and disappointments of his career as a knight-errant. Just as he had foreseen in part 1, chapter 2, his adventures have found a chronicler who has turned them into a book that many of the people he meets in part 2 have read. It is, of course, not at all the kind of book Don Quixote had imagined. He himself seems to have no interest in reading it, probably for the same reasons—a combination of prudence and fear—that keep him from testing his helmet a second time after the first test smashes it (1.1.75). It is because the Duke and Duchess have read about Don Quixote's adventures that they conceive the idea of receiving him as a knight-errant and make him feel for the first time that he really is what he claims to be (2.31.274). The adventures they stage for his benefit afford him an opportunity both to display his bravery by mounting the wooden horse Clavileño, and to defend the honor of Doña Rodríguez's daughter in single combat with the lackey Tosilos. Don Quixote also has an opportunity to demonstrate his fidelity to Dulcinea despite the enticements of Altisidora and, as he at first mistakenly supposes, of Doña Rodríguez as well. He is nevertheless no more satisfied with his new life at the ducal palace than Sancho is with his governorship. Like Aeneas when he forces himself to break away from Dido and leave Carthage for Italy, Don Quixote feels that he has no choice but to get on with his interrupted mission:

Ya le pareció a don Quijote que era bien salir de tanta ociosidad como la que en aquel castillo tenía; que se imaginaba ser grande la falta que su persona hacía en dejarse estar encerrado y perezoso entre los infinitos regalos y deleites que como a caballero andante aquellos señores le hacían, y parecíale que había de dar cuenta estrecha al cielo de aquella ociosidad y encerramiento; y así, pidió un día licencia a los duques para partirse. (2.57.466–67)

(It seemed to Don Quixote that he ought to give up a life of such idleness as he was leading in the castle, for he imagined that he was sorely missed while he remained cloistered and slothful among the countless luxuries and delights that his hosts lavished upon him as a knight-errant, and he felt that he would have to give heaven a strict account of that idleness and seclusion; so one day he asked the Duke and Duchess for permission to leave.)

Perhaps the adventures invented by the Duke and Duchess leave too little scope for Don Quixote's imagination: since they do not need to be transformed by an act of creative will like the random everyday events he encounters earlier, they fail to satisfy the artist in him. Once on the road again in search of further adventures, he praises his restored freedom of action in terms that recall both Sancho's relief at escaping from the constraints of his life as governor of Barataria and Tasso's association of the pastoral life with absolute freedom, though of course without Tasso's erotic overtones:

—La libertad, Sancho, es uno de los más preciosos dones que a los hombres dieron los cielos. . . . Digo esto, Sancho, porque bien has visto el regalo, la abundancia que en este castillo que dejamos hemos tenido; pues en metad de aquellos banquetes sazonados y de aquellas bebidas de nieve, me parecía a mí que estaba metido entre las estrechezas de la hambre, porque no lo gozaba con la libertad que lo gozara si fueran míos; que las obligaciones de las recompensas de los beneficios y mercedes recebidas son ataduras que no dejan campear al ánimo libre. ¡Venturoso aquel a quien el cielo dio un pedazo de pan, sin que le quede obligación de agradecerlo a otro que al mismo cielo!—(2.58.470)

("Liberty, Sancho, is one of the most precious gifts that heaven has bestowed upon men. . . . I say this, Sancho, because you have seen the hospitality and luxury that we have enjoyed in this castle that we are now leaving; yet among those well-seasoned dishes and snow-cooled drinks, I felt as though I were suffering the straits of hunger, since I did not enjoy them as freely as I would have if they had been my own, for the obligation to repay benefits and favors fetters the soul's freedom. Happy is the man to whom heaven has given a bit of bread without the obligation to give thanks for it to anyone except heaven itself!")

The chivalric adventures staged for Don Quixote by the Duke and Duchess turn out to be no more satisfying than his old life as Alonso Quijano had been. That he does not find them more exciting is a sign—perhaps we should say a cause—of his gradual return to sanity, which will be completed only after he returns to his village at the end of part 2.

Sancho, a peasant if not a shepherd, does finally reject ambición, but for much of the book his heart is set on the island Don Quixote has promised him. Teresa shares his ambitions despite her fear that neither her husband nor she herself will be able to meet the demands of their new roles. But Sancho and Teresa do not constitute a threat to the established order; they lack both the intelligence and the social and educational resources that would enable them to make a serious attempt to improve their status. Above all, they lack the driving ambition and the ruthlessness in achieving their goals that characterize an embodiment of the aspiring mind like Macbeth or Marlowe's Tamburlaine. Nor is Don Quixote a serious threat to society, in part because of his madness, but mostly because, like Sancho, he is fundamentally an honest and kindly person. Cervantes does not present either Don Quixote or Sancho as evil. He does ridicule, though not without compassion, their inability to perceive their own limitations.

As in more conventional pastoral works, both Don Quixote and Sancho finally reject the attractions of a courtly life. It is significant that they come to this traditional view—all the more reasonable in the light of their particular experiences at the ducal palace—despite the fact that Don Quixote is a madman, though one blessed with lucid intervals, as Don Diego de Miranda's son observes (2.18.173), and Sancho is an illiterate peasant and not a particularly bright one, "de muy poca sal en la mollera" (1.7.125). Like Ariosto, Cervantes suggests that although men often act foolishly, even the most foolish may sometimes be guided by the light of reason.

CHAPTER VII

Don Quixote's Readers,
Don Quixote as Reader

Don Quixote was an immediate popular success. The first edition, published in Madrid by Juan de la Cuesta in 1605, was followed by nine others, in Madrid, Lisbon, Valencia, Milan, and Brussels, before the appearance of part 2 in Madrid in 1615. The first translation, Thomas Shelton's English version of part 1, appeared in 1607; part 2 followed in 1620. By 1625 translations of both parts were also available in French and Italian (Riley 1986, 174–75). But this popular success did not mean that Cervantes' novel was taken seriously as a work of art. It gave rise to no polemics like those centered on Lope's plays or on the poetry of Góngora (Cherchi 1977, 62). A few remarks made by contemporary writers—among them Lope, Quevedo, and Góngora—suggest that *Don Quixote* did not enjoy much esteem among them, though doubtless some allowance must be made for jealousy caused by the novel's enthusiastic reception. Its very success may have contributed to its being dismissed as a work of "serious" literature. It inspired nothing comparable to the long series of annotated editions in which *Orlando furioso* was read throughout the sixteenth century.

Even if we had contemporary commentaries on *Don Quixote*, we should probably find them as disappointing as the commentaries on *Orlando furioso*. No reader of the sixteenth-century commentaries would suspect that there is anything to laugh at in Ariosto's poem. Unlike most modern critics, the sixteenth-century commentators do not attempt to describe an ideal reader's total response to a text. They try instead to single out elements in the text that can serve as a springboard for further reflection on moral or philosophical questions. We need not suppose that they responded only to the elements they chose to elucidate in their commentaries. And there is, of course, no reason to suppose that all readers would have responded in the same way. Then as now, some readers must have been more able than others to appreciate the originality of a book, less likely to see it simply as a repetition of ideas and attitudes with which they were already familiar.

Renaissance readers believed that their task was to apply a text to their own particular situations, to use it as a source of guidance in shaping their own moral lives. Following Horace's advice in the *Ars Poetica*, they turned to books not just for pleasure but also, and above all, for moral teaching. In terms of the distinction formulated by E. D. Hirsch, Jr. (1967; 1976), they were primarily concerned not with the meaning of the text but with its significance for an individual reader, which need not be the same as its significance for anyone else.

Such a theory of reading is implied in Plutarch's influential essay "How a Young Man Should Study Poetry." Its importance lies in the fact that "alone among the surviving rhetorical classics, Plutarch's emphasis was not on writing or speaking but on reading; not on construction but on interpretation" (Wallace 1974, 277). I know of no sixteenth-century Spanish version of this essay; one of its key points is, however, made also in another essay by Plutarch, translated as "De la poesia y de la utilidad y provecho que se puede sacar de la lection de los Poetas" by Diego Gracián in his volume of selections from the *Moralia* published in Salamanca in 1571:

> Ca bien assi como los buenos medicos qualquier medicina apropriada para una enfermedad conosciendo el vigor y effecto della la passan y aproprian a todas las

enfermedades semejantes: assi tambien qualquier sentencia o razon comun que se puede apropriar para otros usos no conviene dexarla asida a una sola cosa, sino moverla y traspassarla a todo lo proximo semejante y acostumbrar los mancebos a parar mientes en esta proximidad y que traspassen de presto lo proprio en lo comun y premeditar y exercitarse en muchos exemplos para ello. (folio 236 verso)

This passage, like many of Plutarch's other key points in "How a Young Man Should Study Poetry," was incorporated by Erasmus in his *Parabolae* (Parallels), where we read that "as physicians, when a specific has been discovered for one particular disease, adapt it to all diseases that are related and similar, so it is reasonable to adapt an author's words to various purposes" (1978b, 183). The reader will, of course, be guided in his search for the significance of the text by his conception of the kind of moral teaching he should seek, and this is what Erasmus aims to supply both in the *Parabolae* and in many of his other works.

In another even more influential work, *De duplici copia verborum ac rerum commentarii duo*, Erasmus gives detailed instructions on how a student should use his reading as a storehouse of moral precepts. Written at the request of John Colet for use at Saint Paul's School and first published in Paris by Badius in 1512, *Copia* was widely used as a school text in the sixteenth century; nearly 150 editions had appeared by 1572. In *Copia*, Erasmus is concerned, unlike Plutarch, with training writers rather than readers, but his conception of interpretation is fundamentally the same. He advises the student to compile a book of commonplaces arranged under appropriate headings and to commit them to memory so that they will be available for use in speeches or in written compositions. Erasmus stresses that

Some material can serve not only diverse but contrary uses. . . .

The death of Socrates can be used to show that death holds no fear for a good man, since he drank the hemlock so cheerfully; but also to show that virtue is prey to ill will and far from safe amidst a swarm of evils; or again that the study of philosophy is useless or even harmful unless you conform to general patterns of behaviour.

. . . [Socrates] deserves praise for showing such a courageous contempt for death when condemned for no fault of his own but purely out of animosity; he is to be blamed inasmuch as by his useless pursuit of philosophy and disregard of accepted standards he caused bitter grief to his friends, disaster to his wife and children, and destruction to himself (1978a, 639).

There is no Spanish version of *Copia* that might have been accessible to Cervantes. The point is, however, of secondary importance, both because Cervantes might have known the Latin text and because a number of sixteenth-century Spanish works teach the method of reading exemplified by Erasmus' demonstration of the many different moral lessons to be drawn from Plato's account of the death of Socrates. One such work is Fray Miguel de Salinas' *Rhetorica en lengua castellana*, the first and for many years after its publication in 1541 the only manual of rhetoric available in Spanish (Russell 1978). Fray Miguel incorporates a substantial portion of Erasmus' discussion of the moral lessons to be drawn from the death of Socrates. He introduces it this way:

Quiero poner otro exemplo a este effecto y no mas porque es largo y se puede aplicar a muchos titulos conveniblemente. El qual trata Erasmo repartiendole y apropiandole a diversas materias. y bastara para ver en quantas cosas se pueda usar de un exemplo si se saben del aprovechar. Es de la muerte de Socrates. (1541, folio cvi)

(I want to give only one more example of this point since it is long and can be applied appropriately to many different subjects. It comes from Erasmus, who analyzes and applies it to many different matters. And it will suffice to show how many different ways one can use an example if one knows how. It deals with the death of Socrates.)

Fray Miguel repeats the same point two pages later at the end of the passage:

Deste exemplo baste esto para conoscer a quantos propositos se pueden aprovechar de un exemplo si saben y se quieren detener a mirar las particularidades. Para ello ayudara mucho en cada persona de que se haze mencion mirar las circunstancias todas y luego vera si compete aquel exemplo en otras personas en quien concurren las mismas circunstancias. (folio cvii verso)

(Let this example suffice to show how a single example may be adapted to many different subjects if one knows how to do it and if one pays attention to its particular qualities. It will help greatly to do this if one examines the special circumstances of each person mentioned so that one can determine whether the example applies to other persons who find themselves in the same circumstances.)

Like Erasmus, Fray Miguel says nothing about Plato's intentions in telling how Socrates met his end. As John M. Wallace has noted,

> The question whether the meaning we find in a text was
> put there by the author or is foisted on him by ourselves
> bothered Renaissance readers less than it disturbs us ...
> because the answer really did not matter very much. . . .
> Once the explicatory process had begun, then the reader
> was involved for his own good, and it was immaterial
> (or only occasionally material) whether one reader's in-
> terpretation were the same as another's, or identical
> with the author's aims. (1974, 275)

This is true even of the subtlest and most original of all
sixteenth-century readers, Montaigne, for whom, as Steven
Rendall has observed, "the interpreter's quest for definitive
meaning is pernicious ... because it diverts us from the
practical and moral benefits to be derived from reading"
(1979, 1062).

Sixteenth-century critics do not defend Ariosto's use of a
multiple plot by arguing that the various strands are intended
to throw light upon one another; they are not much concerned with demonstrating the relationship between the
whole work and each of its parts. Rather, they want to demonstrate the moral benefit that the reader may gain by con-
templating the parts singly and applying the lessons learned
to the circumstances of his own life. Don Quixote similarly
tries to imitate individual incidents in the life of one of his
heroes—Amadís' madness or his writing a letter to Oriana—
rather than his life as a whole.

The piecemeal interpretation found in the sixteenth-century commentaries is well suited to works, like *Orlando furioso*, made up of a number of analogous actions not always
related very rigorously as cause and effect. Michael Murrin
suggests that this type of structure reflects the common Renaissance practice of reading literary works aloud to a group
of listeners:

Ariosto's episodic tale was recited in parts, the whole being much too long for a single recitation. . . . Spenser could anticipate a segmented understanding of his complex epic and did not have to tidy up his story. His audience would remember certain episodes and certain characters, but they could never be expected to recall the details of his plot. . . . The most an allegorical poet could do was to impose a loose thematic unity on his story. . . . What he could anticipate in his audience was a general understanding of the main narrative thread and an intense concentration on individual episodes and this is precisely what Renaissance commentaries reveal: either an elaborate discussion of individual events or an overall concern for the total myth. (1969, 73)

The practice of reading aloud to a company of listeners did not end with the advent of printing. Books did become less expensive, and it was sometimes possible to borrow them, rent them, or buy them cheaply at estate sales (Bennassar 1982, 264), but they were still far more expensive than they are today: "No labourer in seventeenth-century Europe could readily afford a *book*" (Cruickshank 1978, 812). Even more important must have been the delights of reading as a social pastime, beautifully evoked by Margit Frenk:

Indeed, what a difference there is between hearing a poem and reading it silently, between hearing and reading a novella, a play, a colloquy or any other sort of text! *To hear it* was to perceive it with one's five senses, since one was in direct contact with the person who recited it or read it or narrated it or sang it; one was aware of his presence, of his living voice, his gestures, and of the presence of the other listeners. *To read it* was to be alone with the dead voice of the letters on the page; it was to

read alone and only to read [*era leer solo y sólo leer*].
(1982, 1:122)

The innkeeper's account to Don Quixote's companions of
the harvesters who spend their evenings listening to one of
their companions read aloud from a romance of chivalry
(1.32.393) may have a firm basis in fact (Frenk 1982, 1:116;
Chartier 1986, 155–56). It was not just those too poor to buy
books and those too ignorant to read them for themselves
who listened to them read aloud. In France, at the court of
Francis I, both the choice of reading material and the task of
reading it aloud and commenting on it were assigned to a
special official, the *lecteur ordinaire du roi*; in England, Ariosto's translator, John Harington, read part of a canto of his
work to King James and proudly recalled that the King
praised his performance; in Italy, Ariosto himself entertained
Isabella Gonzaga, who was recovering from childbirth, for
two days in 1507 by reading to her from his still unfinished
Orlando furioso (Nelson 1976–1977, 113–16). The practice of
reading literary works aloud to a group of aristocratic listeners was equally widespread in Spain (Frenk 1982, 1:107–08).

Many features of *Don Quixote* become easier to understand
if we consider it as a work designed to be read aloud to a
group of listeners, though we need not assume that it was
intended to be read exclusively or even primarily this way.
Margit Frenk notes that most of the chapters of Cervantes'
novel are short and tend to be of equal length, as are those
of many romances of chivalry. She suggests that Cervantes
may have divided his work in this way to facilitate oral
presentation, in which it was important not to tax the listeners' power of concentration. She notes also (ibid., 1:109) that
Cervantes ends one chapter with the words "comenzó a decir
lo que oirá y verá el que le oyere o viere el capítulo siguiente"
(2.25.239) (he began to say what the listener or reader will

hear or read in the following chapter) and begins another with the epigraph "Que trata de lo que verá el que lo leyere, o lo oirá el que lo escuchare leer" (2.66.541) (which deals with the matters that the reader will see or the listener will hear).

An author who expects his work to be read aloud must pay special attention to local effects, even at the expense of the overall composition of his work. *Don Quixote* incorporates a large number of jokes and witty anecdotes, many of them drawn from oral tradition. Modern readers are inclined to ask what bearing such stories have on the central themes of the novel or what they reveal about the personalities of its characters. Sometimes, indeed, the stories do enrich our understanding, as does the story Don Quixote tells Sancho when the latter expresses surprise that Dulcinea del Toboso, whom he had taken to be a princess, is in reality the peasant girl Aldonza Lorenzo:

> Has de saber que una viuda hermosa, moza, libre y rica, y sobre todo, desenfadada, se enamoró de un mozo motilón, rollizo y de buen tono; alcanzólo a saber su mayor, y un día dijo a la buena viuda por vía de fraternal reprehensión:—"Maravillado estoy, señora, y no sin mucha causa, de que una mujer tan principal, tan hermosa y tan rica como vuestra merced, se haya enamorado de un hombre tan soez, tan bajo y tan idiota como fulano, habiendo en esta casa tantos maestros, tantos presentados y tantos teólogos, en quien vuestra merced pudiera escoger como entre peras, y decir: Éste quiero, aquéste no quiero—". Mas ella le respondió, con mucho donaire y desenvoltura:— "Vuestra merced, señor mío, está muy engañado, y piensa muy a lo antiguo si piensa que yo he escogido mal en fulano, por idiota que le parece; pues para lo que yo le quiero, tanta filosofía sabe,

y más, que Aristóteles—". Así que, Sancho, por lo que
yo le quiero a Dulcinea del Toboso, tanto vale como la
más alta princesa de la tierra. (1.25.313)

(I would have you know that a pretty widow, young,
independent, rich, and above all free and easy in her
conduct, fell in love with a strapping good-humored
young lay brother. His superior found out about it and
one day he said to the worthy widow as a sort of broth-
erly reproach: "I am surprised, my lady, and rightly so,
that a woman of such high social position, and one so
fair and so rich as you are, has fallen in love with a man
as common, low, and stupid as So-and-so when there
are in this house so many masters, graduates, and theo-
logians from whom you might choose like so many
pears, saying "This one I'll take, that one I won't." But
she answered him with perfect composure: "My lord,
you are very much mistaken and very old-fashioned if
you think I've made a bad choice in So-and-so, however
stupid he seems to you, since for what I want from him
he knows as much philosophy as Aristotle, and more."
So you see, Sancho, that for my purposes Dulcinea del
Toboso is as good as the finest princess on earth.)

In this case Don Quixote himself explains the significance of
the anecdote, though many modern readers will feel that the
explanation itself is psychologically revealing in a way that
Don Quixote surely does not intend it to be. Seventeenth-
century readers are more likely to have seen the anecdote
simply as a funny story, though one told with unusual grace
and verve. This is still more apt to have been the case when
the story is only loosely tied to the plot or to one of the
principal characters, like the story of the painter Orbaneja
that Don Quixote recalls on two occasions, first (2.3.63–64) in
order to demonstrate that "no ha sido sabio el autor de mi

historia" since he had included the story of "El curioso impertinente" which has nothing to do with Don Quixote himself, and a second time in order to disparage the author of the
apocryphal part 2 (2.71.574). It is true, as Márquez Villanueva
points out (1973, 169), that Cervantes usually incorporates his
anecdotes in a way that the compilers of jokebooks and collections of stories did not. But he does not always do so, and
his contemporaries may have been more inclined than we are
to enjoy the stories for themselves without asking what they
have to do with the novel as a whole.

Like the innumerable proverbs and popular sayings cited
by Sancho and others, the jokes and anecdotes incorporated
in *Don Quixote* give Cervantes' novel something of the quality of the miscellanies and compilations of heterogeneous information so popular in the Renaissance, books like Pero
Mexía's *Silva de varia lección*. First published in 1540, Mexía's
Silva was reprinted more than thirty times in the sixteenth
century, and was translated into several languages, including
French, Italian and English. The miscellanies doubtless owed
some of their enormous popularity to the ease with which
they lent themselves to the social pastime of oral reading.
Lady Anne Clifford reports in her diary that "upon the 9th
[November 1616] I sat at my work and heard Rivers and
Marsh read Montaigne's [*Essays*] which book they have read
almost this fortnight" (quoted in Nelson 1976–1977, 116).

The miscellanies were popular in part because they could
claim, with some justification, to offer both a stimulus to
moral reflection and useful information on a variety of topics.
Though the Canon of Toledo denounces the romances of
chivalry for their many absurdities, he is willing to concede
that they do have one redeeming feature: the opportunity
they offer a writer to demonstrate his learning in the most
varied fields and thus both to delight and instruct his readers
(1.47.566–67).

Don Quixote itself has some of the qualities of a miscellany. Several of the interpolated novellas in part 1 can be detached from their context in the novel and read as autonomous works. Indeed, both "El curioso impertinente" and the story of Marcela and Grisóstomo were translated into French and published separately before the appearance of César Oudin's version of part 1 in 1614. As Maxime Chevalier notes, "it is as if seventeenth-century readers performed a vivisection on *Don Quixote* part 1, dividing it into the burlesque misadventures of a minor nobleman and his simpleminded squire on the one hand and the romantic adventures of 'El curioso impertinente' or those of Luscinda, Dorotea, Cardenio and Don Fernando on the other" (1981, 121).

The fondness of Renaissance readers for miscellanies is reflected also in their delight in "treasuries" or *florilegia* drawn from narrative works. The florilegia also served the practical purpose of providing a store of material that the reader could use in his own writings or in conversation. Orazio Toscanella appended to his *Bellezze del "Furioso"* (1574) a list of passages from Ariosto's poem intended to be used in precisely this way. The list is unpaged and provided with a separate title page and a preface "Ai lettori," perhaps an indication that it was also issued separately. In the preface, Toscanella explains that his selection of commonplaces (*luochi communi*) will be a great help to his readers both in speaking and in writing, "cosí nel parlare, come nello scrivere," and will greatly enhance their reputations. The commonplaces are useful because they can be adapted to many different situations provided one knows how to apply them to the matter at hand:

> poi che le particolari attioni, & cose particolari, da i luochi communi derivano, come fiumi da fonti: & chi ha cognitione de i luochi communi, può a propositi partico-

lari, servirsi di loro; & con lo aiuto loro, le occorrenti particolarità trattare ottimamente ... cosí essi ... detti a buon proposito, faranno onore. Et scrivendo ancora (pur che l'huomo sappia far di verso prosa; & sappia imitare) nelle orationi, ne i discorsi, & in qualunque cosa occorra loro conforme, & connaturale; torneranno à giovamento incredibile; & à maravigliosa gloria.

Don Quixote uses *Amadís de Gaula* and *Orlando furioso* in exactly the way the florilegia were designed to foster. Not, of course, only the florilegia, for, as E. C. Riley observes, "When [Don Quixote] sets out to imitate his incredible heroes ... his reaction is only an exaggerated instance of that which heroic literature was supposed to provoke" (1962, 106). Don Quixote, of course, was not alone in trying to model his life on the romances of chivalry. Sir Philip Sidney asserts in his *Defense of Poetry* that he has known men who were moved to practice courtesy, liberality, and above all courage by reading *Amadís*. Saint Ignatius Loyola, while recovering from the wounds he received defending Pamplona against the French in 1521, resolved to dedicate himself to the service of God and to perform deeds worthy of Saint Francis of Assisi, Saint Dominic and Amadís. Though Loyola, like Juan de Valdés and Juan Luis Vives, later denounced his affection for the romances of chivalry as a youthful aberration, it has been suggested that his reading of the romances may have inspired him to found the Jesuit Order (Whinnom 1967, 18). Similarly, Charles V's decision to give up his throne in favor of his son Philip II and to retire to the monastery of Yuste has been seen as an imitation of Lisuarte's handing over of his throne to Amadís (Jones 1971, 56).

Don Quixote's error is not that he tries to model his life on books, or even that he chooses the wrong kind of books, though of course he might have chosen better ones. Marthe

Robert is surely right in saying that "Don Quixote's adventures would scarcely be affected if, instead of devouring nonsensical romances, he gorged himself as immoderately on sacred books" (1977, 59). Don Quixote's error is that he follows his models too literally. He fails to realize something every major Renaissance critic accepted without question: a successful imitation must not follow its original slavishly.

This conception of imitation is not confined to treatises on rhetoric. In Castiglione's *Book of the Courtier* Count Ludovico da Canossa declares that if Virgil had imitated Hesiod in everything he would not have surpassed him, "se Virgilio avesse in tutto imitato Esiodo, non gli serìa passato inanzi" (1.37.146). This is a special case of the general principle, announced by Messer Federigo Fregoso in book 2, that one's actions should always be appropriate to oneself and to one's position in life:

> Voglio adunque che 'l nostro cortegiano in ciò che egli faccia o dica usi alcune regole universali.... Consideri ben che cosa è quella che egli fa o dice e 'l loco dove la fa, in presenza di cui, a che tempo, la causa perché la fa, la età sua, la professione, il fine dove tende e i mezzi che a quello condur lo possono; e così con queste avvertenzie s'accommodi discretamente a tutto quello che fare o dir vole. (2.7.199–200)

> (Therefore, in all that he does or says I would have our courtier follow certain general rules.... Let him consider well what he does or says, the place where he does it, in whose presence, its timeliness, the reason for doing it, his own age, his profession, the end at which he aims, and the means by which he can reach it; thus, keeping these points in mind, let him act accordingly in whatever he may choose to do or say [Singleton 1959, 98].)

Federigo makes the connection between this point and the doctrine of imitation explicit a little later when he says that

> Ad ognun non si convien ogni cosa.... Bisogna che ognun conosca se stesso e le forze sue ed a quello s'accommodi, e consideri quali cose ha da imitare e quali no. (2.20.221–22)

> (Not everything is suited to everybody.... Everyone must know himself and his own powers, and govern himself accordingly, and consider what things he ought to imitate and what things he ought not [Singleton 1959, 114].)

Don Quixote repeats Federigo's precept in the excellent advice he gives Sancho when the latter is about to take up his post as governor of Barataria: "has de poner los ojos en quien eres, procurando conocerte a ti mismo, que es el más difícil conocimiento que puede imaginarse" (2.42.357) (you must keep your eyes fixed on who you are and try to know yourself, which is the hardest kind of knowledge to acquire).

Don Quixote himself, of course, does not practice what he preaches. He fails to adapt the precepts he draws from his reading to his own situation in life, not that of a youthful knight-errant but that of a middle-aged nobleman of moderate means. The rewards he expects from his labors, like the labors themselves, are far beyond his reach. Though he does achieve fame, it is not at all the kind of fame he sought. E. C. Riley has noted that "Part I had 'commemorated' [Don Quixote] not as he wished to be commemorated, but as he was—as a man who took himself, and who wished to be taken, for other than he was" (1962, 204). It is this, and not his desire for fame, that is his undoing. A. A. Parker is too harsh when he says that Don Quixote's "ideal, noble in itself, has been warped from the start by pride and ambition" (1956, 6).

The promise of easy triumphs Don Quixote finds in his reading reaches Sancho secondhand and makes him dream of becoming governor of a province or ínsula. Cervantes reproaches the romances of chivalry for depicting a world like Ariosto's, a "fine insidious world where heroism is not necessary" (Greene 1963, 143) and for doing so without the corrective of Ariosto's irony. The romances are dangerous because they make the path of virtue seem easy. They are dangerous also because they suggest that the very real virtues they celebrate—loyalty, courage, generosity—belong to a world wholly unlike the ordinary world inhabited by their readers. "Don Quixote's reading has taught him that heroism is something extravagant and fantastic," writes A. A. Parker. "This is the bad thing about the romances of chivalry: they do not bear witness to truth" (1948, 296). There is a sense in which *Don Quixote* really is what Cervantes' anonymous friend in the prologue to part 1 says it is: an attack on the romances of chivalry. But it is also something more. George Haley has noted that "in proposing to discredit the chivalric novel, Cervantes does not suggest that we not read chivalric novels, but only that we read them properly for what they are, outlandish and sometimes beautiful lies, fiction rather than history" (1965, 164). *Don Quixote* is an attack on a way of reading—not just of reading the romances of chivalry, but of reading itself. Cervantes' true subject is the interaction between books and their readers.

CONCLUSION

More than thirty years ago, Northrop Frye protested against "the sloppy habit of identifying fiction with ... the novel" (1957, 303). Ten years later Robert Scholes and Robert Kellogg were still complaining that "our view of narrative literature is almost hopelessly novel-centered" (1966, 8). Today the situation has changed, as Gerald Prince's useful *Dictionary of Narratology* (1987) makes clear. Thanks to the work of writers like Vladimir Propp (1968), Mikhail Bakhtin (1981) and Gérard Genette (1980), discussions of narrative no longer deal almost exclusively with the novel, nor even with prose fiction. As Seymour Chatman (1978) and others have noted, stories need not be told in words; a silent film or a ballet may present some of the same features that characterize a prose narrative. Whether a story is told in prose or in verse is of secondary importance.

Cervantes' contemporaries certainly thought so. The Canon of Toledo, whose comments have often been taken as an expression of Cervantes' own views, insists that verse is not an essential attribute of epic, "que la épica también puede escrebirse en prosa como en verso" (1.47.567).

But of course the Canon, like everyone who read *Don Quixote* when it was first published, could have had no idea of the future development of the kind of prose fiction that we know as the novel. To see *Don Quixote* as belonging to the tradition that Ian Watt calls the novel of formal realism is to approach it with expectations that it cannot sustain. Most of the interpolated stories do not deal with what Robert Alter has seen as the hallmark of most serious fiction, "an intent, verisimilar representation of moral situations in their social contexts" (1975, ix). The physical settings of Cervantes' novel, those Castilian roads so often evoked by modern critics, are not treated realistically. As Vladimir Nabokov notes, Cervantes' landscapes usually present "a tame world of conventional brooks and invariable green meadows and pleasant woods, all made to man's measure or improved by man," not "the wild, bitter, sunstunned, frozen, parched, tawny, brown pinedark mountains of Spain" (1983, 33–34). Though Flaubert's thematic debt to *Don Quixote* in *Madame Bovary* is evident, Ariosto provides a better preparation for appreciating the style and structure of *Don Quixote*.

Above all, Ariosto provides an excellent basis for understanding Cervantes' unique blending of the serious and the comic. A. A. Parker has remarked that "the best of the Spanish picaresque novelists were engaged, as was Cervantes in *Don Quixote*, in breaking down the barrier between the comic and the serious" (1967, 26). This is true enough, but it is worth noting that Ariosto had already broken down that barrier in *Orlando furioso* and in ways that have more to do with Cervantes' practice in *Don Quixote* than do the works of the picaresque novelists. *Don Quixote* is nevertheless much more than a reworking of *Orlando furioso*, much more even than a synthesis of all the books from which Cervantes learned his craft. Reading the book he wrote in the light of some of the books he read reveals how well he assimilated the lesson Don Quixote failed to learn: that mere copying is not true imitation.

We cannot read *Don Quixote* as its first readers did, and we would not want to if we could. There is no doubt that Cervantes' contemporaries failed to perceive, let alone appreciate, many qualities of his masterpiece that seem to us most evident and most valuable: "To claim that Cervantes' contemporaries understood his purpose is to leap to a conclusion that not only belies his remarks about his readers but is also contradicted by our own reading of Avellaneda's inability to capture the essence of *Don Quixote*" (Weiger 1985, 233). Alban K. Forcione has stressed the relevance for *Quixote* criticism of the distinction, made in current theories of the aesthetics of reception, between the immediate meaning of a literary work and its potential meaning: "the *Quixote* is the preeminent case of a literary work that, before it can become fully meaningful, requires a profound alteration in its public, a process which can unfold in decades or centuries and which can in some instances be effected by the powers of its own imaginative energy" (1982, 16).

At the same time, we must recognize that Cervantes, like everyone else, was a product of his own time. He shared with his contemporaries views on the nature and proper function of literature that often go counter to those generally held today. *Don Quixote* was a popular success, as Cervantes must have hoped. There is ample reason to suppose that he tried to give his readers what he thought they wanted, though surely he also tried to give them more. I hope the preceding pages have demonstrated the importance of knowing something about the books with which both Cervantes and his first readers were familiar. I hope they have also demonstrated the importance of undertaking the difficult task of discovering how those old books were read when they were still new.

BIBLIOGRAPHY

Primary Sources

Ariosto, Ludovico. 1553. *Orlando furioso*. Trans. Jerónimo de Urrea. Venice: Gabriel Giolito.

———. 1556. *Orlando furioso*. Ed. Girolamo Ruscelli. Venice: Vincenzo Valgrisi.

———. 1562. *Orlando furioso*. Ed. Girolamo Ruscelli and Nicolò Eugenico. Venice: Vincenzo Valgrisi.

———. 1570. *Orlando furioso*. Ed. Lodovico Dolce and Thomaso Porcacchi. Venice: Domenico and Giovanni Battista Guerra.

———. 1970. *"Orlando furioso" raccontato da Italo Calvino con una scelta del poema*. Turin: Einaudi.

———. 1974. *Orlando furioso*. Trans. Guido Waldman. London: Oxford University Press.

———. 1975–77. *Orlando furioso*. Trans. Barbara Reynolds. 2 vols. Harmondsworth: Penguin.

———. 1981. *Orlando furioso*. Ed. Lanfranco Caretti. Turin: Einaudi.

———. 1982. *Orlando furioso*. Ed. Emilio Bigi. 2 vols. Milan: Rusconi.

Castiglione, Baldesar. 1955. *"Il cortegiano" con una scelta delle opere minori*. Ed. Bruno Maier. Turin: Unione Tipografico-Editrice Torinese.

———. 1959. *The Book of the Courtier*. Trans. Charles S. Singleton. Garden City N.Y.: Anchor-Doubleday.

Cerda, Juan de la. 1599. *Libro intitulado, vida politica de todos los estados de mugeres*. Alcalá de Henares: Juan Gracián.

Cervantes Saavedra, Miguel de. 1987. *La Galatea*. Ed. Juan Bautista Avalle-Arce. Madrid: Espasa-Calpe.

———. 1978. *El ingenioso hidalgo Don Quijote de la Mancha*. Ed. Luis Andrés Murillo. 3 vols. Madrid: Castalia.

———. 1981. *Don Quixote*. Trans. John Ormsby; revised by Joseph R. Jones and Kenneth Douglas. New York: W. W. Norton.

————. 1982. *Novelas ejemplares*. Ed. Juan Bautista Avalle-Arce. 3 vols. Madrid: Castalia.

Covarrubias, Sebastián de. 1943. *Tesoro de la lengua castellana o española*. Ed. Martín de Riquer. Barcelona: Horta.

Dante Alighieri. 1970–75. *The Divine Comedy*. Ed. and trans. Charles S. Singleton. 3 vols. Princeton: Princeton University Press.

Diccionario de autoridades. *See* Real Academia Española.

Erasmus, Desiderius. 1978a. *"Copia": Foundations of the Abundant Style*. Trans. and annotated Betty I. Knott. In *Collected Works of Erasmus*, vol. 24, *Literary and Educational Writings*, ed. Craig R. Thompson, 279–660. Toronto: University of Toronto Press.

————. 1978b. *Parallels*. Trans. and annotated R. A. B. Mynors. In *Collected Works of Erasmus*, vol. 23, *Literary and Educational Writings*, ed. Craig R. Thompson, 123–277. Toronto: University of Toronto Press.

Fórnari, Simon. 1549. *Spositione . . . sopra l'"Orlando furioso."* Florence: Lorenzo Torrentino.

González de Cellorigo, Martín. 1600. *Memorial de la politica necesaria y util restauracion à la Republica de España*. Valladolid: Juan de Bostillo.

León, Fray Luis de. 1951. *La perfecta casada*. In *Obras completas castellanas*, 2d ed, ed. P. Félix García, O.S.A., 233–342. Madrid: Editorial Católica.

Luxán, Pedro de. 1552. *Coloquios matrimoniales . . . En los quales se trata como se han de aver entre si los casados*. Seville: Juan Canalla.

Mexía, Vicente. 1566. *Saludable instrucion del estado de matrimonio*. Córdoba: Juan Vicente Escudero.

The Oxford English Dictionary Being a Corrected Re-issue . . . of "A New English Dictionary on Historical Principles." 1933. 13 vols. Oxford: Clarendon Press.

Petrarca, Francesco. 1976. *Petrarch's Lyric Poems: The "Rime sparse" and Other Lyrics*. Trans. and ed. Robert M. Durling. Cambridge: Harvard University Press.

Plutarch. 1571. *Morales de Plutarco*. Trans. Diego Gracián. Salamanca: Alexandro de Cánova.

Real Academia Española. 1726–39. *Diccionario de la lengua castellana*. 6 vols. Madrid.

Salinas, Fray Miguel de. 1541. *Rhetorica en lengua castellana*. Alcalá de Henares: Juan de Brocar.

Sidney, Sir Philip. 1962. *Poems*. Ed. William A. Ringler, Jr. Oxford: Clarendon Press.

Tasso, Torquato. 1966. *Opere*. Ed. Giorgio Petrocchi. Milan: Ugo Mursia.

Thomas Aquinas, Saint. 1975. *Summa theologiae*, vol. 38 (2a2ae. 63–79). Ed. and trans. Marcus Lefébure O. P. London: Eyre and Spottiswoode in conjunction with Blackfriars.

Toscanella, Orazio. 1574. *Bellezze del "Furioso" di M. Lodovico Ariosto ... con gli argomenti et allegorie de i canti*. Venice: Pietro de i Franceschi, & nepoti.

Virgil. 1934. *Aeneid*. Ed. and trans. H. Rushton Fairclough. 2d ed. Cambridge: Harvard University Press.

SECONDARY SOURCES

Allen, Don Cameron. 1970. *Mysteriously Meant: The Rediscovery of Symbolism and Allegorical Interpretation in the Renaissance*. Baltimore: Johns Hopkins Press.

Alpers, Paul J. 1967. *The Poetry of "The Faerie Queene."* Princeton: Princeton University Press.

Alter, Robert. 1975. *Partial Magic: The Novel as a Self-conscious Genre*. Berkeley: University of California Press.

Auerbach, Erich. 1949. *Introduction aux études de philologie romane*. Frankfurt am Main: Vittorio Klostermann.

———. 1951. "Die verzauberte Dulcinea." *Deutsche Vierteljahrsschrift für Literaturwissenschaft und Geistesgeschichte* 25:294–316.

———. 1953a. "Epilegomena zu *Mimesis*." *Romanische Forschungen* 65:1–18.

———. 1953b. *Mimesis: The Representation of Reality in Western*

Literature. Trans. Willard R. Trask. Princeton: Princeton University Press.

————. 1965. *Literary Language and Its Public in Late Latin Antiquity and the Middle Ages.* Trans. Ralph Manheim. New York: Bollingen Foundation.

Bakhtin, M. M. 1981. *The Dialogic Imagination.* Ed. Michael Holquist; trans. Caryl Emerson and Michael Holquist. Austin: University of Texas Press.

Barber, C. L. 1959. *Shakespeare's Festive Comedy: A Study of Dramatic Form and Its Relationship to Social Custom.* Princeton: Princeton University Press.

Bataillon, Marcel. 1950. *Erasmo y España: Estudios sobre la historia espiritual del siglo XVI.* Trans. Antonio Alatorre. 2 vols. Mexico City: Fondo de Cultura Económica.

Bigi: see Ariosto 1982 in Primary Sources.

Bennassar, Bartolomé. 1982. *Un Siècle d'or espagnol, 1525–1648.* Paris: Robert Laffont.

Borges, Jorge Luis. 1960. "Kafka y sus precursores." In *Otras inquisiciones*, 145–48. Buenos Aires: Emecé.

Brand, C. P. 1974. *Ludovico Ariosto: A Preface to the "Orlando furioso."* Edinburgh: Edinburgh University Press.

Brenan, Gerald. 1953. *The Literature of the Spanish People: From Roman Times to the Present Day.* 2d ed. Cambridge: Cambridge University Press.

Brownlee, Marina Scordilis. 1985. "Cervantes as Reader of Ariosto." In *Romance: Generic Transformation from Chrétien de Troyes to Cervantes*, ed. Kevin Brownlee and Marina Scordilis Brownlee, 220–37. Hanover, N.H.: University Press of New England.

Calvino: see Ariosto 1970 in Primary Sources.

Caretti: see Ariosto 1981 in Primary Sources.

Carne-Ross, D. S. 1966. "The One and the Many: a Reading of *Orlando furioso*, Cantos 1 and 8." *Arion* 5: 195–234 [continued as "The One and the Many: A Reading of *Orlando furioso*" *Arion*, n.s. 3 (1977): 146–219].

Cave, Terence. 1979. *The Cornucopian Text: Problems of Writing in the French Renaissance.* Oxford: Clarendon Press.

Chartier, Roger. 1986. "Les pratiques de l'écrit." In *Histoire de la vie privée*, vol. 3, *De la renaissance aux lumières*, ed. Roger Chartier, 113–61. Paris: Éditions du Seuil.

Chatman, Seymour. 1978. *Story and Discourse: Narrative Structure in Fiction and Film*. Ithaca, N.Y.: Cornell University Press.

Cherchi, Paolo. 1977. *Capitoli di critica cervantina (1605–1789)*. Rome: Bulzoni.

Chevalier, Maxime. 1966. *L'Arioste en Espagne (1530–1650): Recherches sur l'influence du "Roland furieux."* Bordeaux: Institut d'Études Ibériques et Ibéro-américaines de l'Université de Bordeaux.

———. 1975. *Cuentecillos tradicionales en la España del siglo de oro*. Madrid: Gredos.

———. 1976. *Lectura y lectores en la España de los siglos XVI y XVII*. Madrid: Turner.

———. 1978. *Folklore y literatura: El cuento oral en el siglo de oro*. Madrid: Gredos.

———. 1981. *"Don Quichotte* et son public." In *Livre et lecture en Espagne et en France sous l'ancien régime: Colloque de la Casa de Velázquez*, 119–25. Paris: Éditions A.D.P.F.

Close, Anthony. 1978. *The Romantic Approach to "Don Quixote": A Critical History of the Romantic Tradition in "Quixote" Criticism*. Cambridge: Cambridge University Press.

Colie, Rosalie. 1974. *Shakespeare's Living Art*. Princeton: Princeton University Press.

Cruickshank, D. W. 1978. " 'Literature' and the Book Trade in Golden-Age Spain." *Modern Language Review* 73:799–824.

Davis, Walter R. 1969. *Idea and Act in Elizabethan Fiction*. Princeton: Princeton University Press.

De Blasi, Giorgio. 1952–53. "L'Ariosto e le passioni." Parts 1–2. *Giornale storico della letteratura italiana* 129: 318–62; 130: 178–203.

Delcorno Branca, Daniela. 1973. *L'"Orlando furioso" e il romanzo cavalleresco medievale*. Florence: Leo S. Olschki.

Devoto, Daniel. 1960. "Folklore et politique au Château Ténébreux." In *Les fêtes de la Renaissance*, vol. 2, *Fêtes et cérémonies au temps de Charles V*, ed. Jean Jacquot, 311–29. Paris: Centre National de la Recherche Scientifique.

Dolce: see Ariosto 1570 in Primary Sources.

Domínguez Ortiz, Antonio. 1971. *The Golden Age of Spain, 1516–1639*. Trans. James Casey. London: Weidenfeld and Nicolson.

Dunn, Peter M. 1972. "Two Classical Myths in *Don Quixote*." *Renaissance and Reformation* 9:2–11.

Durling, Robert M. 1965. *The Figure of the Poet in Renaissance Epic*. Cambridge: Harvard University Press.

Elliott, J. H. 1963. *The Revolt of the Catalans: A Study in the Decline of Spain (1598–1640)*. Cambridge: Cambridge University Press.

———. 1977. "Self-Perception and Decline in Early Seventeenth-Century Spain." *Past and Present*, no. 74: 41–61.

Empson, William. 1935. *Some Versions of Pastoral*. London: Chatto and Windus.

Farrell, R. B. 1977. *Dictionary of German Synonyms*. 3rd ed. Cambridge: Cambridge University Press.

Fergusson, Francis. 1975. "The *Poetics* of Aristotle." In his *Literary Landmarks: Essays on the Theory and Practice of Literature*, 3–36. New Brunswick, N.J.: Rutgers University Press.

Forcione, Alban K. 1970. *Cervantes, Aristotle and the "Persiles."* Princeton: Princeton University Press.

———. 1982. *Cervantes and the Humanist Vision: A Study of Four "Exemplary Novels."* Princeton: Princeton University Press.

Foster, George M. 1965. "Peasant Society and the Image of Limited Good." *American Anthropologist* 67:293–315.

Fowler, Alastair. 1982. *Kinds of Literature: An Introduction to the Theory of Genres and Modes*. Cambridge: Harvard University Press.

Frenk, Margit. 1982. " 'Lectores y oidores': La difusión oral de la literatura en el siglo de oro." In *Actas del Séptimo Congreso de la Asociación Internacional de Hispanistas celebrado en Venecia del 25 al 30 de agosto de 1980*, 1:101–23. 2 vols. Rome: Bulzoni.

Frye, Northrop. 1957. *Anatomy of Criticism: Four Essays*. Princeton: Princeton University Press.

BIBLIOGRAPHY

Genette, Gérard. 1980. *Narrative Discourse: An Essay in Method*. Trans. Jane E. Lewin. Ithaca: Cornell University Press.

———. 1982. *Palimpsestes: la littérature au second dégré*. Paris: Éditions du Seuil.

Gerhardt, Mia Irene. 1955. *"Don Quijote": La vie et les livres*. Amsterdam: Noord-Hollandsche Uitgevers Maatschappij; Mededelingen der Koninklijke Nederlandse Akademie van Wetenschappen, Afd. Letterkunde, n.s. part 18, no. 2:17–57.

Greene, Thomas. 1963. *The Descent from Heaven: A Study in Epic Continuity*. New Haven: Yale University Press.

Haley, George. 1965. "The Narrator in *Don Quijote*: Maese Pedro's Puppet Show." *MLN* 80:145–65.

Hart, Thomas R. 1977. "The Pilgrim's Role in the First *Solitude*." *MLN* 92:213–26.

———. 1981. "Versions of Pastoral in Three *Novelas ejemplares*." *Bulletin of Hispanic Studies* 58:283–91.

———. 1984. "Insight and Method: Erich Auerbach." In *Literary Theory and Criticism: Festschrift in Honor of René Wellek*, ed. Joseph P. Strelka, 1:249–65. 2 vols. Bern: Peter Lang.

Hart, Thomas R. and Steven Rendall. 1978. "Rhetoric and Persuasion in Marcela's Address to the Shepherds." *Hispanic Review* 46:287–98.

Heartz, Daniel. 1960. "Un divertissement de palais pour Charles V à Binches." In *Les fêtes de la Renaissance*, vol. 2, *Fêtes et cérémonies au temps de Charles V*, ed. Jean Jacquot, 329–42. Paris: Centre National de la Recherche Scientifique.

Hendrix, W. S. 1925. "Sancho Panza and the Native Comic Types of the Sixteenth Century." In *Homenaje ofrecido a Menéndez Pidal*, 2:485–94. 3 vols. Madrid: Hernando.

Herrero, Javier. 1978. "Arcadia's Inferno: Cervantes' Attack on Pastoral." *Bulletin of Hispanic Studies* 55:289–99.

Hirsch, E. D., Jr. 1967. *Validity in Interpretation*. New Haven: Yale University Press.

———. 1976. *The Aims of Interpretation*. Chicago and London: University of Chicago Press.

Javitch, Daniel. 1988. "Narrative Discontinuity in the *Orlando Furioso* and Its Sixteenth-Century Critics." *MLN* 103:50–74.

Jones, R. O. 1966. "Bembo, Gil Polo, Garcilaso: Three Accounts of Love." *Revue de littérature comparée* 40:526–40.

———. 1971. *The Golden Age: Prose and Poetry.* Vol. 2, *A Literary History of Spain,* ed. R. O. Jones. London: Ernest Benn.

Kelso, Ruth. 1956. *Doctrine for the Lady of the Renaissance.* Urbana: University of Illinois Press.

Köhler, Erich. 1966. "Wandlungen Arkadiens: die Marcela-Episode des *Don Quijote* (I, 11–14)." In *Esprit und arkadische Freiheit: Aufsätze aus der Welt der Romania,* 302–27. Frankfurt am Main: Athenäum.

Kroeber, A. L. 1948. *Anthropology.* New York: Harcourt, Brace.

Levin, Harry. 1957. "The Example of Cervantes." In *Contexts of Criticism,* 79–96. Cambridge: Harvard University Press.

Lewis, C. S. 1936. *The Allegory of Love.* Oxford: Clarendon Press.

———. 1942. *A Preface to "Paradise Lost."* London: Oxford University Press.

Lisón Toledano, Carmen. 1966. *Belmonte de los Caballeros: A Sociological Study of a Spanish Town.* Oxford: Clarendon Press.

Lloréns, Vicente. 1967. "La intención del *Quijote.*" In *Literatura, historia, política,* 205–22. Madrid: Revista de Occidente.

———. 1974. "*Don Quijote* y la decadencia del hidalgo." In *Aspectos sociales de la literatura española,* 47–66. Madrid: Castalia.

McGaha, Michael D. 1980. "Cervantes and Virgil." In *Cervantes and the Renaissance,* ed. Michael D. McGaha, 34–50. Newark, Delaware: Juan de la Cuesta.

McKendrick, Melveena. 1974. *Women and Society in the Spanish Drama of the Golden Age: A Study of the "mujer varonil."* Cambridge: Cambridge University Press.

McKeon, Michael. 1987. *The Origins of the English Novel 1600–1740.* Baltimore: Johns Hopkins University Press.

Maclean, Ian. 1980. *The Renaissance Notion of Woman.* Cambridge: Cambridge University Press.

Mancing, Howard. 1982. *The Chivalric World of "Don Quijote": Style, Structure and Narrative Technique.* Columbia: University of Missouri Press.

Mandel, Oscar. 1958. "The Function of the Norm in *Don Quixote.*" *Modern Philology* 55:154–63.

Maravall, José Antonio. 1976. *Utopía y contrautopía en el "Quijote."* Santiago de Compostela: Pico Sacro.

Márquez Villanueva, Francisco. 1973. *Fuentes literarias cervantinas.* Madrid: Gredos.

————. 1975. *Personajes y temas del "Quijote."* Madrid: Taurus.

Murrin, Michael. 1969. *The Veil of Allegory: Some Notes Toward a Theory of the Allegorical Epic in the English Renaissance.* Chicago: University of Chicago Press.

Nabokov, Vladimir. 1983. *Lectures on "Don Quixote."* Ed. Fredson Bowers. New York: Harcourt Brace Jovanovich.

Nelson, William. 1973. *Fact or Fiction: The Dilemma of the Renaissance Storyteller.* Cambridge: Harvard University Press.

————. 1976–77. "From 'Listen, Lordings' to 'Dear Reader'." *University of Toronto Quarterly* 46:110–24.

Parker, A. A. 1948. "El concepto de la verdad en el *Quijote.*" *Revista de filología española* 32:287–305.

————. 1956. "Fielding and the Structure of *Don Quixote.*" *Bulletin of Hispanic Studies* 33:1–16.

————. 1967. *Literature and the Delinquent: The Picaresque Novel in Spain and Europe 1599–1753.* Edinburgh: Edinburgh University Press.

Pigman, G. W., III. 1980. "Versions of Imitation in the Renaissance." *Renaissance Quarterly* 33:1–32.

Poggioli, Renato. 1975. *The Oaten Flute: Essays on Pastoral Poetry and the Pastoral Ideal.* Cambridge: Harvard University Press.

Prince, Gerald. 1987. *A Dictionary of Narratology.* Lincoln: University of Nebraska Press.

Propp, Vladimir. 1968. *Morphology of the Folktale.* 2d ed. Trans. Laurence Scott. Austin: University of Texas Press.

Redfield, Robert 1956. *Peasant Society and Culture.* Chicago: University of Chicago Press.

Redondo, Agustín. 1978. "Tradición carnavalesca y creación literaria del personaje de Sancho Panza al episodio de la ínsula Barataria en el *Quijote.*" *Bulletin Hispanique* 80:39–70.

Rendall, Steven. 1979. "*Mus in Pice*: Montaigne and Interpretation." *MLN* 94:1056–71.

Riley, E. C. 1962. *Cervantes's Theory of the Novel.* Oxford: Clarendon Press.

————. 1986. *Don Quixote*. London: Allen and Unwin.

Riquer, Martín de. 1973. "Cervantes y la caballeresca." In *Suma cervantina*, ed. J. B. Avalle-Arce and E. C. Riley, 273–92. London: Támesis.

Robert, Marthe. 1977. *The Old and the New: From "Don Quixote" to Kafka*. Trans. Carol Cosman. Berkeley and Los Angeles: University of California Press.

Russell, P. E. 1969. *"Don Quixote* as a Funny Book." *Modern Language Review* 64:312–26.

————. 1978. "Un libro indebidamente olvidado—la *Retorica en lengua castellana* (1541) de Fray Miguel de Salinas." In *Libro-homenaje a Antonio Pérez Gómez*, 2:130–41. 2 vols. Cieza, Murcia: La Fonte que Mana y Corre.

————. 1985. *Cervantes*. Oxford: Oxford University Press.

Salza, Abd-el-Kader. 1914. *Studi su Ludovico Ariosto*. Città di Castello: S. Lapi.

Scholes, Robert and Robert Kellogg. 1966. *The Nature of Narrative*. New York: Oxford University Press.

Segre, Cesare. 1966. "Un repertorio linguistico e stilistico dell' Ariosto: la *Commedia*." In *Esperienze ariostesche*, 51–83. Pisa: Nistri-Lischi.

Singleton: see Castiglione 1959 in Primary Sources.

Smith, Hallett. 1952. *Elizabethan Poetry: A Study in Conventions, Meaning, and Expression*. Cambridge: Harvard University Press.

Trevor-Roper, Hugh. 1976. *Princes and Artists: Patronage and Ideology at Four Habsburg Courts*. New York: Harper and Row.

Tuve, Rosemond. 1966. *Allegorical Imagery: Some Mediaeval Books and Their Posterity*. Princeton: Princeton University Press.

Vilar, Jean-Pierre. 1967. "Don Quijote arbitrista (Sobre la reformación en tiempos de Cervantes)." *Beiträge zur romanischen Philologie* sonderheft: 124–29.

Vilar, Pierre. 1956. "Le temps du Quichotte." *Europe* 34:3–16.

Vinaver, Eugene. 1971. *The Rise of Romance*. Oxford: Clarendon Press.

Wallace, John M. 1974. " 'Examples Are Best Precepts': Readers and Meanings in Seventeenth-Century Poetry." *Critical Inquiry* 2:273–90.

Wardropper, Bruce W. 1982. "La eutrapelia en las *Novelas ejemplares* de Cervantes." In *Actas del Séptimo Congreso de la Asociación Internacional de Hispanistas celebrado en Venecia del 25 al 30 de agosto de 1980*, 1:153–69. 2 vols. Rome: Bulzoni.

Watt, Ian. 1957. *The Rise of the Novel*. Berkeley and Los Angeles: University of California Press.

Weiger, John G. 1985. *The Substance of Cervantes*. Cambridge: Cambridge University Press.

Weinberg, Bernard. 1961. *A History of Literary Criticism in the Italian Renaissance*. 2 vols. Chicago: University of Chicago Press.

Weisser, Michael R. 1973. "The Decline of Castile Revisited: The Case of Toledo." *Journal of European Economic History* 2:614–40.

———. 1976. *The Peasants of the Montes: The Roots of Rural Rebellion in Spain*. Chicago: University of Chicago Press.

Whinnom, Keith. 1967. *Spanish Literary Historiography: Three Forms of Distortion*. Exeter: University of Exeter.

———. 1980. "The Problem of the 'Best-Seller' in Spanish Golden-Age Literature." *Bulletin of Hispanic Studies* 57:189–98.

Yates, Frances A. 1975. *Astraea: The Imperial Theme in the Sixteenth Century*. London: Routledge and Kegan Paul.

INDEX

INDEX

INDEX

PRINCETON ESSAYS IN LITERATURE

The Orbit of Thomas Mann
By Erich Kahler

*On Four Modern Humanists: Hofmannsthal, Gundolf,
Curtius, Kantorowicz*
Edited by Arthur R. Evans, Jr.

Flaubert and Joyce: The Rite of Fiction
By Richard Cross

A Stage for Poets: Studies in the Theatre of Hugo and Musset
By Charles Affron

Hofmannsthal's Novel "Andreas"
By David H. Miles

Kazantzakis and the Linguistic Revolution in Greek Literature
By Peter Bien

Modern Greek Writers
Edited by Edmund Keeley and Peter Bien

On Gide's Prométhée: Private Myth and Public Mystification
By Kurt Weinberg

The Inner Theatre of Recent French Poetry
By Mary Ann Caws

Wallace Stevens and the Symbolist Imagination
By Michel Benamou

Cervantes' Christian Romance: A Study of "Persiles y Sigismunda"
By Alban K. Forcione

*The Prison-House of Language: A Critical Account of
Structuralism and Formalism*
By Fredric Jameson

Ezra Pound and the Troubadour Tradition
By Stuart Y. McDougal